ROUGH MAGIC

Jezebel

Mark Cantan

Published by Playdead Press 2014

© Mark Cantan 2014

Mark Cantan has asserted his rights under the Copyright, Design and Patents Act, 1988, to be identified as the author of this work.

A CIP catalogue record for this book is available from the British Library.

ISBN 978-1-910067-20-8

Caution
All rights whatsoever in this play are strictly reserved and application for performance should be sought via The Lisa Richards Agency 33 Old Compton Street, London W1D 5JU before rehearsals begin. No performance may be given unless a licence has been obtained.

This book is sold subject to the condition that it shall not by way of trade or otherwise, be lent, resold, hired out, or otherwise circulated without the publisher's prior consent in any form of binding or cover other than that in which it is published and without a similar condition including this condition being imposed on the subsequent purchaser.

Printed by BPUK

Playdead Press
www.playdeadpress.com

Jezebel
by Mark Cantan
Soho Theatre, 12-31 August 2014

Cast (in alphabetical order)
Alan	Peter Daly
Robin	Margaret McAuliffe
Jezebel	Valerie O'Connor
Director	Lynne Parker
Director – Original Production	José Miguel Jiménez
Set & Lighting Designer	Ciarán O'Melia
Costume Designer	Deirdre Dywer
Dramaturg	Maureen White
Production Manager	Rob Furey
Stage Directors	Justin Murphy
	Stephanie Ryan
Graphic Design	Stuart Bradfield
Photography	Patricio Cassinoni
	Lucy Nuzum
Video	Mark Cantan
Publicist	Nancy Poole
Producers	Diego Fasciati
	Clare Robertson

Jezebel was first performed at Project Arts Centre, Dublin on 8 December 2012.

Mark Cantan

Mark was a participant on Rough Magic's SEEDS programme 2010-2011, during which he received a commission to write *Jezebel*, which was produced at Project Arts Centre in December 2012 and won the Stewart Parker Trust New Playwright Bursary.

Mark started writing as well as acting while studying Maths (the perfect qualification for a writer) at Trinity College Dublin. Since graduating he has worked in any medium that will take him; writing for theatre, TV, radio, magazines, and the medium that just can't say no: the internet. He has written and co-directed a feature film called *The Alarms: A Story in Words* as well as a production of his play, *The Get Together*. Recently he completed a commission for the Abbey Theatre called *The Big Bad Wolf*, contributed *Somewhere* to Fishamble's *Tiny Plays for Ireland II* and wrote the script for RTÉ's hidden camera sitcom *Baptism of Hire*. Currently he is participating in Six in the Attic, an Irish Theatre Institute Initiative.

As well as writing he also performs regularly as part of comedy improv team *Goose* and has just finished his first solo album available at markcantan.bandcamp.com. He really enjoys earning money so if you would like to pay him some don't hesitate to get in touch. He wrote this biog but weirdly likes talking about himself in the third person.

For more information check out www.markcantan.com.

ROUGH MAGIC

Since its foundation in 1984 Rough Magic has built an organisation based on three core values: artistic excellence, an egalitarian approach to the creative ensemble and an ethic based on pluralism. The company has evolved around the principle that we are part of a world culture that can celebrate Irish identity diverse in nature and outward looking in its vision.

Jezebel, winner of the Stewart Parker Trust New Playwright Bursary for 2012, was developed during Mark Cantan's participation in Rough Magic's SEEDS programme and produced by the company in 2012. Mark's play is a modern Comedy of Manners, in the best tradition of some of Rough Magic's greatest influences, from Sheridan to Stoppard. Like them, he uses the comic potential of language and situation to explore our world and the absurdities of the human condition. *Jezebel* is a piece of forensic observation; smart, satisfying and very funny.

Rough Magic's policy has three strands; commissioning new Irish work, presenting the best of contemporary international writing and innovative productions from the classical repertoire. Our work includes over 50 Irish and world premieres and the debuts of many Irish theatre-makers. Based in Dublin, we regularly perform at Project Arts Centre, and tour in Ireland, the UK and beyond, garnering many awards, both at home and abroad.

In addition, we are active in the development of new theatre artists. Our SEEDS programme, now in its twelfth year, is the benchmark for professional development in Irish theatre and the only one of its kind. In 2011 we launched ADVANCE, a parallel programme for established artists, and through our Production Support, which provides participants with a range of practical assistance, mentoring and resource-sharing opportunities, we enable the work of many individual artists and emerging companies.

Through these strategic initiatives, the richness of its artistic ambition and its national and international reach, Rough Magic is connected to theatre activity in Ireland across the full spectrum of experience and creative practice. Our aim is firstly to make great theatre, but also to advance and contribute to our culture. We will continue to put the artist at the centre of our production and development structures; to build on our position as a national company; and to form supportive partnerships with organisations and individuals who share our sense of the unique value of art, particularly theatre, in offering a new vision for the nation.

For further information visit www.roughmagic.ie

For Rough Magic

Artistic Director	Lynne Parker
Executive Producer	Diego Fasciati
Producer/Artist Development	Clare Robertson
Dramaturg	Maureen White
Associate Directors	Sophie Motley
	Matt Torney
Accountant	Katy Falkingham

Board of Directors
Marie Redmond (Chair)
William Earley
Anne Fogarty
Roy Foster
Darragh Kelly
Stephen McManus
Sheila O'Donnell
Jill Percival
Gerry Smyth

Advisory Council
Siobhán Bourke
Anne Byrne
Catherine Donnelly
Declan Hughes
Darragh Kelly
Pauline McLynn
Hélène Montague
Martin Murphy
Arthur Riordan
Stanley Townsend

SEEDS Artists
Cait Corkery
Daniel Forde
Shane Mac an Bhaird
Cameron Macaulay
Zoe Ní Riordáin

Independent Producer in Residence
Jen Coppinger

Production Support
Rough Magic Production Support is a resource sharing initiative designed to support individual artists and emerging companies. Through this programme, Rough Magic shares its office facilities and offers practical advice and mentoring at no cost to the participants. Current and past participants include: Annie Gill, ANU Productions, Sarah Baxter & Kate Heffernan, Bright Light Productions, Denis Clohessy, Collapsing Horse Theatre Company, Shaun Dunne & Talking Shop Ensemble, Christine Dwyer Hickey, Making Strange Theatre Company, Zoe Ní Riordáin, Pageant Wagon, Playgroup, Aoife Spillane-Hinks, TheEmergencyRoom, Then This Theatre, Dylan Tighe, Trees Rd Productions, Underscore_Productions and Willfredd Theatre.

Rough Magic gratefully acknowledges the support of the Arts Council/An Comhairle Ealaíon, Culture Ireland, our Patrons and Dublin City Council.
Registered Number: 122753

Rough Magic Theatre Company
18 South Great George's Street, Dublin 2, Ireland
Tel: +353 (0)1 671 9278
Email: info@roughmagic.ie
Web: www.roughmagic.ie

London's most vibrant venue for new theatre, comedy and cabaret.

Soho Theatre is a major creator of new theatre, comedy and cabaret. Across our three different spaces we curate the finest live performance we can discover, develop and nurture. The company works with theatre makers and companies in a variety of ways, from full producing of new plays, to co-producing new work, working with associate artists and presenting the best new emerging theatre companies that we can find. We have numerous writers and theatre makers on attachment and under commission, six young writers and comedy groups and we read and see hundreds of shows a year – all in an effort to bring our audience work that amazes, moves and inspires.

'Soho Theatre was buzzing, and there were queues all over the building as audiences waited to go into one or other of the venue's spaces. [The audience] is so young, exuberant and clearly anticipating a good time.' *Guardian*

We attract over 170,000 audience members a year. We produced, co-produced or staged over forty new plays in the last twelve months. Our social enterprise business model means that we maximise value from Arts Council and philanthropic funding; we actually contribute more to government in tax and NI than we receive in public funding.

sohotheatre.com

Keep up to date:
sohotheatre.com/mailing-list
facebook.com/sohotheatre
twitter.com/sohotheatre
youtube.com/sohotheatre

Registered Charity No: 267234

Soho Theatre, 21 Dean Street, London W1D 3NE
sohotheatre.com
Admin 020 7287 5060 | Box Office 020 7478 0100

SOHO STAFF

Artistic Director Steve Marmion
Executive Director Mark Godfrey

BOARD OF DIRECTORS
Nicholas Allott (chair)
Sue Robertson (vice chair)
Oladipo Agboluaje
David Aukin
Hani Farsi
Beatrice Hollond
Shappi Khorsandi
Jeremy King
Lynne Kirwin
Neil Mendoza
Carolyn Ward
Roger Wingate
Christopher Yu

HONORARY PATRONS
Bob Hoskins – President
Peter Brook CBE
Simon Callow
Gurinder Chadha
Sir Richard Eyre CBE

ARTISTIC TEAM
Associate Director Nina Steiger
Creative Producer Rebecca Gould
Writer's Centre &
Education Co-ordinator Julia Haworth
Casting Director Nadine Rennie CDG
Comedy & Cabaret Producer Steve Lock
Comedy Assistant Sarah Dodd
Theatre Producer David Luff
Assistant Producer Lauren Mackintosh
Associate Producer
Comedy & Cabaret Lee Griffiths
Artistic Associate Suzanne Gorman
Artistic Associate Joe Murphy
Resident Assistant Director Josh Roche
Channel 4 Playwright Clara Brennan
Resident Composer Greg Harradine

ADMINISTRATION
General Manager Catherine McKinney
Executive Assistant Rose Abderabbani
Financial Controller Kevin Dunn
Finance Officer Kate Wickens
Finance Assistant Hattie Davis
Business Development Director
Jacqui Gellman
Administrator
Amy Smith (maternity leave)
Administrator Anna Williams

COMMUNICATIONS
Marketing Manager Beccy Rimmer
Marketing Officer Jen Pearce
Marketing Assistant Myles Cook
Press & PR Manager Michael Eppy
Press Assistant Judi Ellard
Graphic Designer
Michael Windsor-Ungureanu
Graphic Design Assistant Joe Hales
Project Development Associate
Sam Hansford

DEVELOPMENT
Development Director James Atkinson
Development Manager Livvy Brinson
Development Assistant Joana Rodrigues

BOX OFFICE
AND FRONT OF HOUSE
Operations Manager Julie Marshall
Box Office Manager Melinda Liu
Deputy Box Office Manager Paul Carroll
Box Office Supervisors
Amanda Collins, Molly White
Box Office Assistants
Fuad Ahammed, Lainey Alexander, Grace Barry, Victor Correia, Eniola Jaiyeoba, Teddy Lamb, Alan Stratford, Molly White
Customer Managers
Maider Lacalle, Nika Obydzinski
Duty & Venue Managers
Nick Comley, Janet Downer, Lucy Frost, Ian Irvine, Rebecca Keable-Crouch, Caggy Kerlogue, Maider Lacalle, Nika Obydzinski
Front of House Staff
Clare Andrews, Emma Akwako, Rose Adolph, Brenton Arrendell, Bob Dobson, Claire Louise English, John Hewer, Hayat Kamil, Teddy Lamb, Aryana Ramkhalawon, Daniel Rosenberg, Alice Sillett, Abi Symons, Misheck Williams, Jasmine Woodcock-Stewart

PRODUCTION
Technical Manager Nick Blount
Deputy Technical Manager Greg Borrell
Senior Technician Eve D'Alton
Technician Paolo Melis
Technician Bex Keable-Crouch
Freelance Technicians Paolo Carlotto, Juan Carmona, Rob Foskett, Dan Williams

THANK YOU

We are immensely grateful to our fantastic Soho Theatre Friends and Supporters. Soho Theatre is supported by Arts Council England. This theatre has the support of the Channel 4 Playwrights' Scheme sponsored by Channel 4 Television.

Principal Supporters
Nicholas Allott
Hani Farsi
Jack and Linda Keenan
Amelia and Neil Mendoza
Lady Susie Sainsbury
Carolyn Ward
Jennifer and Roger Wingate

The Soho Circle
Celia Atkin
Giles Fernando
Michael and Jackie Gee
Hedley and Fiona Goldberg
Isobel and Michael Holland

Corporate Sponsors
Bates Wells & Braithwaite
Cameron Mackintosh Ltd
Caprice Holdings Ltd
Dusthouse
Financial Express
Fisher Productions Ltd
Fosters
Granta
The Groucho Club
Hall & Partners
John Lewis Oxford Street
Latham & Watkins LLP
Left Bank Pictures
London Film Museum
Nexo
Oberon Books Ltd
Overbury Leisure
Ptarmigan Media
Publicis
Quo Vadis
Soho Estates
Soundcraft
SSE Audio Group

Trusts & Foundations
The Andor Charitable Trust
Backstage Trust
Boris Karloff Charitable Foundation
Bruce Wake Charitable Trust
The Buzzacott Stuart Defries Memorial Fund
The Charles Rifkind and Jonathan Levy Charitable Settlement
The City of Westminster Charitable Trust
The Coutts Charitable Trust
The David and Elaine Potter Foundation
The D'Oyly Carte Charitable Trust
The Ernest Cook Trust
The Edward Harvist Trust
The 8th Earl of Sandwich Memorial Trust
Equity Charitable Trust
The Eranda Foundation
Esmée Fairbairn Foundation
The Fenton Arts Trust
The Foundation for Sport and the Arts
The Foyle Foundation
Harold Hyam Wingate Foundation
Help A London Child
Hyde Park Place Estate Charity
The Ian Mactaggart Trust
John Ellerman Foundation
John Lewis Oxford Street Community Matters Scheme
John Lyon's Charity
The John Thaw Foundation
JP Getty Jnr Charitable Trust
The Kobler Trust
The Mackintosh Foundation
The Mohamed S. Farsi Foundation
The Rose Foundation
Rotary Club of Westminster East
The Royal Victoria Hall Foundation
Sir Siegmund Warburg's Voluntary Settlement
St Giles-in-the-Fields and William Shelton Educational Charity
The St James's Piccadilly Charity
Teale Charitable Trust
The Theatres Trust
The Thistle Trust
Unity Theatre Charitable Trust
Westminster City Council-West End Ward Budget
The Wolfson Foundation

Soho Theatre Best Friends
Nick Bowers
Johan and Paris Christofferson
Richard Collins
Miranda Curtis
Cherry and Rob Dickins
Norma Heyman
Beatrice Hollond
David King
Lady Caroline Mactaggart
Jesper Nielsen and Hannah Soegaard-Christensen
Hannah Pierce
Suzanne Pirret
Amy Ricker
Ian Ritchie and Jocelyne van den Bossche
Ann Stanton
Alex Vogel
Garry Watts
Phil and Christina Warner
Sian and Matthew Westerman
Hilary and Stuart Williams

Soho Theatre Dear Friends
Natalie Bakova
Quentin Bargate
Norman Bragg
Neil and Sarah Brener
Jonathan Glanz
Jane Henderson
Anya Hindmarch and James Seymour
Shappi Khorsandi

Jeremy King
Michael Kunz
James and Margaret Lancaster
Anita and Brook Land
Nick Mason
Annette Lynton Mason
Andrew and Jane McManus
Mark and Carolyn Mishon
Mr & Mrs Roger Myddelton
Karim Nabih
James Nicola
Lauren Prakke
Phil and Jane Radcliff
Sir Tim Rice
Sue Robertson
Dominic and Ali Wallis
Nigel Wells
Andrea Wong
Matt Woodford
Christopher Yu

Soho Theatre Good Friends
Oladipo Agboluaje
Jed Aukin
Jonathan and Amanda Baines
Mike Baxter
David Brooks
Indigo Carnie
Chris Carter
Benet Catty
Jeremy Conway
Sharon Eva Degen
David Dolman
Geoffrey and Janet Eagland
Gail and Michael Flesch
Sue Fletcher
Daniel and Joanna Friel
Stephen Garrett, Kudos Films
Alban Gordon
Doug Hawkins
Tom Hawkins
Thomas Hawtin
Etan Ilfeld
Steve Kavanagh
Pete Kelly
Lynne Kirwin
Lorna Klimt
David and Linda Lakhdhir
Charlotte MacLeod
Amanda Mason
Mike Miller
Ryan Miller
Glyn Morgan
Catherine Nendick
Martin Ogden
Alan Pardoe
David Pelham
Fiona and Gary Phillips
Dan Savidge
Barry Serjent
Lesley Symons
Dr Sean White
Liz Young

We would also like to thank those supporters who wish to stay anonymous as well as all of our Soho Theatre Friends.

Jezebel
Mark Cantan

Characters:

Alan
Robin
Jezebel

ROBIN, a woman in her early thirties with a ready-for-business pony tail and ready-for-drinks suit, and ALAN, a man in his early thirties wearing practical glasses and a quiet suit, speak kindly to each other.

ALAN: Listen...

ROBIN: Look...

ALAN: This has been great...

ROBIN: I really like you...

Both: but...

ALAN: I don't think this is going to work out.

ROBIN: I'm just not sure there's a future here.

ALAN: If you really need a reason I guess it's partly, that you keep sleeping with other guys.

ROBIN: Mostly because you're kind of racist. Against Irish people.

ALAN: You're sort of full on Trish.

ROBIN: You're kind of complicated Colm.

ALAN: You're a little jealous Julie.

ROBIN: You lack a bit of motivation Jack.

ALAN: I just haven't built up the same tolerance for alcohol as you have. Or the same tolerance for fist fighting.

ROBIN: To be honest I haven't understood half of the words that you've said to me. In the nicest possible way, it's like I'm dating a cryptic crossword.

ALAN: No, honestly, it's nothing to do with your family. Please, please don't tell them that, Jane. Particularly not your brother.

ROBIN: I think you'd be happier with someone else, Cian. Someone with really, *really* large breasts.

ALAN: I feel like we've run out of things to say to each other... [*Looks for a response.*] Right? ...Haven't we? ...Patricia?

ROBIN: I guess I'm more into guys who *don't* have an underground bunker Steve.

ALAN: I find it kind of grating to hear the sound of your laughter, Elaine, when you see old people just walking along the street.

ROBIN: I just need some time alone Jim. Well, not alone obviously - but with *less* people in my life. One less. You.

ALAN: I'm sorry this hasn't worked out Charlotte. But it was fun. And

	informative; to see the inside of a morgue, so many times.
ROBIN:	Where I am, in my life, right now, I'm just not looking to get married, to you and your three brothers. That's just where I'm at.
ALAN:	Sometimes you've just got to know when it's time to quit while you're ahead, cash your chips and walk away from the poker table. And I'm not just talking about your chronic gambling addiction.

ROBIN and ALAN arrive at a café table at the same time.

ALAN:	Oh, sorry. You go ahead.
ROBIN:	No, it's fine. You take it.
ALAN:	No, please. The person I'm waiting for hasn't arrived yet so...
ROBIN:	Nor has min- Unless you're Alan?
ALAN:	Oh. Yes. Robin?
ROBIN:	Well, that works out perfectly then.
ALAN:	Beautiful.

They sit. Both are flustered by each other.

ALAN:	I mean, the coincidence. Is beautiful.
ROBIN:	Yes.

ALAN: Although you are too. Don't get me wrong.

ROBIN: Oh. Thanks. Well, I must say I'm impressed. With your stuff. Your statistics. The statistical analysis that you did for Aoife. Not your vital stat...

ALAN: Uh, thanks. Yes, it was very nice of Aoife to pass me on to you. My details.

ROBIN: She had nothing but good things to say about you. When I told her I was looking for someone she said you were the man for me. Uh, for my statistical needs.

ALAN: Aoife was great. I mean, she is great. I mean, I was delighted I could give her what she wanted. Needed. I mean, she was very amenable. I mean, her company is. It was a pleasure appraising her. Her inputs and outputs. That she has as a single individ-...a sole trader.

ROBIN: [*Dumbstruck for a second before regaining herself.*] Yes, absolutely. Uhm, so. More importantly. What do you want to do with me? For me! To me! Sorry, everything sounds wrong now. Can we start again?

ALAN: Absolutely.

ROBIN: Great. Should we go out?

ALAN: On a date?

ROBIN: And come in again.

ALAN: Oh, yes, sorry. I thought you were asking me out.

ROBIN: No, no, no. Absolutely not!

ALAN: [*Slightly disappointed.*] Oh.

ROBIN: I mean I'm not saying absolutely not. But I'd put you in an awkward position if I asked you out. I mean metaphorically. Not physically. I'm not particularly into awkward positions.

ALAN: No, I wasn't thinking that... before. [*Pictures the awkward positions.*]

ROBIN: It would be a weird thing to bring up in a meeting.

ALAN: I guess so.

ROBIN: Unless we agreed that I wouldn't base my decision on the contract on it.

ALAN: Right.
On the meeting?

ROBIN: On the date.

ALAN: Right.
Uh...

ROBIN:	Whether you wanted to go on one or not. That wouldn't affect my decision.
ALAN:	Good.
ROBIN:	I mean, you seem like a suitable candidate.
ALAN:	Oh, thanks.
ROBIN:	Pro-active, macro-focused, goal divisive, nice arms. So are you up for it?
ALAN:	Sure. Wait. Which?
ROBIN:	What?
ALAN:	Are you talking about the contract or the date?
ROBIN:	The date. I think. Wait. Which are you saying "sure" to?
ALAN:	Either. Both. If you're keen then I am. I'd love to get into your area.
ROBIN:	Okay. Wait, what...?
ALAN:	Of business. Your area of business. The motivational books and the positivity lectures and stuff. I'm a big fan of that kind of thing. I didn't mean your... uhm... Not that I wouldn't. I'm sure... it's... very...

ROBIN: [*Trying to help him.*] Yes, of course. Right. Absolutely. Well, I certainly like it.

ALAN: Your...?

ROBIN: My area of business.

ALAN: Yes.
Great.
So we're going on a date then?

ROBIN: Yes.
Great.
I think so.

Both think about it to make sure they've got it straight in their heads.

JEZEBEL, a woman in her late twenties wearing a dizzying assortment of arty clothes, watches them.

JEZEBEL: [*To Audience.*] Well. It seemed like Alan and Robin were meant for each other. Which they were. But they didn't know that yet. They just felt like it. If you know what I mean. Kind of. Wait, do *I* know what I mean? Hold on let me think about this for a second. I'll get back to you.

ALAN: Hey.

ROBIN: Hi.

ALAN: I can't believe you've turned up. Table for two please.

ROBIN: What, why? I'll have the Cheng Du Chicken.

ALAN: Oh, I just... I mean, clearly you're a 7 when, averaging out all my previous girlfriends and taking the result as a reflexive indicator, I'm only a 6. Well, actually, in truth, the numbers come to 5.4 but I tend to remove Nuala Norris as an anomalous data point because I was very young when I was with her. And she was very old. Can we get the bill?

ROBIN: Two for Play It By Fear please. I hope it didn't seem too impulsive the other day. Some girls want a guy to prove his undying love 20 times over before they'll even meet his eye without snarling. But I'm more of a trial and error, have a go kind of person. It's always worth a shot. If they like you great. If not, well, it's been a learning experience. Apart from that one guy who wanted to get a guide dog so he could text while he was walking. I learned nothing from that encounter. Oh my god that film had the most unbelievable ending I've ever seen.

ALAN: Here *we* go, Mojitos. [*Hands her a drink.*] Y'know "sensible" is like a bad word these days but to me it's one of the most attractive things in a person. No games, no pretending to not be interested, no unreal expectations, no wanting me to be some mythical hero who knows exactly how to sweep a woman off her feet. Which Nuala made me promise to never actually attempt again after I hit her head on that side table. G&T for me? G&T for ye?

ROBIN: Usually you can tell if it's not going to work out pretty soon into the date. He'll be intimidated by my career orientation, or suspicious of my forthrightness, or not impressed with my work-life balance. So I'll just pull the plug. There's no point in going on with things if it's not going to work out. Taxi!

JEZEBEL: I mean. Okay. What I'm saying is that, like, they seemed perfect for each other. And they were but... were they, was the question. Well, yes and no, and, I suppose, in a way, no and yes. Otherwise things would've gone very differently. Which they did.

The living room door bursts open and ALAN and ROBIN walk in laughing.

ALAN: Haha.

ROBIN: So I flushed the toilet and that was the end of it.

ALAN: Hahaha.

ROBIN: Haha.

Their laughter ebbs away.

ALAN looks at ROBIN in amazement. He pauses a moment to take her in.

ALAN: Do you like tuna?

ROBIN: Tuna steak or tinned tuna?

ALAN: Tinned tuna.

ROBIN: I can't stand it.

ALAN: Me too.

ALAN kisses ROBIN.

After a moment ROBIN pulls back.

ROBIN: [*Suspicious.*] Are you religious?

ALAN: Not at all.

ROBIN: [*Relieved.*] Okay.

They kiss again and start to move over to the sofa.

ALAN: Do you smoke?

ROBIN: No.

ROBIN is up against the back of the sofa. ALAN kisses her.

ROBIN: Pets?

ALAN: Dogs.

She kisses him.

ALAN: TV?

ROBIN: [*Shakes her head.*] DVD.

ALAN kisses her.

ROBIN: Mushrooms?

ALAN: Never.

ROBIN lies back on the sofa.

ALAN: Travel?

ROBIN looks at ALAN and takes a breath.

ROBIN: Anywhere without a dictatorial system of government or an oppressive foreign policy.

ALAN turns off the light.

JEZEBEL is standing, talking on the phone.

JEZEBEL: I just can't believe this, Gringo. How could you not tell me *this* is what you do for a living?

ROBIN: Jezebel: In a way her destiny was sealed from birth.

JEZEBEL: Well, yes, okay, yes, you *said* it but you didn't- ...you should have been more clear. I thought you meant *art* dealer. We were standing in a gallery.

ROBIN: Her parents decided to call her Jezebel because they wanted to reclaim what they considered to be a beautiful, melodic name that had strangely gone out of fashion. Which is laudable, in a way.

JEZEBEL: I don't know! I just thought you were offering me some mints. I can't keep up with all the names you people have for these things.

ALAN: The name "Jezebel" has a frequency of below 0.001%. Most probably because of the connotations of highly transferable affections.

JEZEBEL: Yes, okay, fine. Now I know; "Brain Tork isn't a type of mint." I have it written down.

ROBIN: As soon as she hit 18 she immediately self-actioned her desire focus by applying to change it by deed-poll.

JEZEBEL: [*Deflates.*] Five years Gringo. Even with good behaviour it's a long time. What are we going to do?

ALAN: Unfortunately she got confused by the forms and ended up just putting down the same name again.

JEZEBEL: You know I'll stand beside you. Well, in front of you anyway, with bullet proof glass between us.

ROBIN: By the time she got to reapply she'd managed to sell a few paintings under her real name changing it seemed counter-productive.

JEZEBEL: What do you mean "maybe that isn't the best idea"?

ROBIN: So she just accepted her destiny.

ALAN: Which was, in fact, the inverse of what her name suggests.

JEZEBEL: See other people? What other people? You're in prison. Wait a second. You're breaking up with me? From prison? You're breaking up with me from prison? ...[*Defeated.*] Well, three weeks may not seem like a very significant relationship to you but it was to me. [*JEZEBEL hangs up the phone and looks up at an unseen till* *operator.*] Oh, sorry, no, I don't have a loyalty card.

JEZEBEL: But then six months into their relationship Alan and Robin had just finished watching an episode of The Sleeping Detective.

ROBIN and ALAN are watching TV. ROBIN presses a button on the remote and turns the TV off. Both talk with forced passion.

ALAN: Well...

ROBIN: Are you in the mood for...?

ALAN: Absolutely. If you'd like.

ROBIN: Oh yes. I think I'm feeling frisky.

ALAN: Oooh, excellent. I... can't wait.

They look at each other. Then ALAN chickens out.

ALAN: Let me just check my email and then I will be all over you.

ALAN looks at his phone.

ROBIN: Come and get me mister.

ALAN puts his phone down again and they turn back to each other. Until ROBIN flakes out.

ROBIN: After I've just texted Justine about lunch tomorrow.

ROBIN takes out her phone.

ALAN: Oh, you'd better go ahead and text because once I'm done with you you won't be able to use that phone your fingers will be trembling so much, with pleasure.

ROBIN: [*Half distracted by texting.*] Wow. I can't wait. So much so I'm not even going to bother to use proper punctuation in this text.

ALAN: Good. You'd better hurry. Because once you've done that I don't think I'll be able to hold myself back any longer. Unless you need to wait for a reply.

ROBIN puts away her phone.

ROBIN: Oh no, no, no. I'm just confirming, Justine won't need to reply so... I am *all* yours. Do with me what you will.

ALAN: You saucy minx. [*Leans awkwardly towards ROBIN.*] Well, I am going to start... by...

ALAN stops and checks his phone again.

ROBIN: Someone ringing?

ALAN: No, sorry, I thought it buzzed but it didn't.

ROBIN: Oh is it doing that thing where it buzzes to tell you that the message has been sent?

ALAN: No, I figured out how to get rid of that.

ROBIN: Oh really?

ALAN starts showing her on his phone.

ALAN: Yeah, it's just in settings, but it sounds like it's talking about a different thing because when you look at it, see, it just says welcome screen so what are you supposed to...

ROBIN looks at ALAN.

ROBIN: Oh Alan. What's gone wrong?

ALAN: Well, I just don't think the message screen is what-

ROBIN: With us.

ALAN: Is there something wrong?

ROBIN: We've only been going out for 6 months surely we should still be all over each other. Instead we're discussing phone settings.

ALAN: Yeah.

ROBIN: I think that maybe we're avoiding the fact that our sex life isn't all that we might want it to be.

ALAN: Yeah, I guess I could kind of tell you weren't really enjoying it either.

ROBIN: We're just all over the place. We're constantly at odds, pulling in different directions.

ALAN: Again I apologise for that. [*Looking at her forehead.*] You can barely see the bump any more.

ROBIN: I meant metaphorically.

ALAN: Oh yeah.

ROBIN: So... what does that mean?

ALAN: Well, we can't go on like this.

They begin to get worried.

ROBIN: We should get some advice from someone.

ALAN: Yes. Who are you thinking?

ROBIN: Justine, Carmel, Sandra?

ALAN: Your friends?! I thought you meant a counsellor or something.

ROBIN: What would a *counsellor* know about our sex life?

ALAN: [*Suspicious.*] Well, what do your friends know about-?

ROBIN: [*Moving swiftly on.*] What about Frank then?

ALAN: [*Shocked.*] Your father?! We can't talk to him. I already feel like whenever I meet him we're both just thinking about the fact that I do it with his daughter without him now knowing that *it* isn't even that good.

ROBIN: Okay, Dermot then.

ALAN: *My* father?! I... no... [*Shudders at the thought of it.*]

ROBIN: Well, do you have any ideas?

ALAN: Maybe some instruction manuals? I mean, it'd take a while for us to write them but...

ROBIN: Maps stress me out a bit.

ALAN: Fair enough. How about... How about... Ummmm... Shortly after breaking up with Gringo Jezebel was in her art studio with her friend Julia.

JEZEBEL wanders around forlornly.

ROBIN: Julia's a classic "glory-mole": The kind of woman who doesn't really care about you except for how you're caring about her.

ALAN: Julia was at work on a stirring new painting which she was daubing with goat's cheese. Jezebel however wasn't being quite so productive.

JEZEBEL sighs heavily and looks to see if Julia has noticed.

JEZEBEL lets out a quiet, mournful moan.

ALAN: Eventually Julia noticed her.

ROBIN: She told Jezebel that she was trying to concentrate so could she please go into another room if she wanted to sing.

JEZEBEL: Gringo broke up with me.

ALAN: Julia was shocked.

ROBIN: She couldn't believe Jezebel was going out with someone.

JEZEBEL: [*Miffed.*] Yes. Gringo, the guy I met at CopyRat's exhibition.

ALAN: Julia was shocked.

ROBIN: She couldn't believe *Jezebel* was going out with someone.

JEZEBEL: Yes. Gringo. I told you all about him. The one that took me on that midnight cruise down the coast.

ALAN: Julia was shocked.

ROBIN: She couldn't believe Jezebel was *going out* with someone.

JEZEBEL: Yes. Gringo. He was planning to take me to Amsterdam.

ROBIN: Julia still couldn't understand why someone was dating Jezebel so she enquired as to whether it was someone that *she* knew.

JEZEBEL: No, he wasn't trying to make *you* jealous by going out with *me*. It's not like the last time. It doesn't matter who he is. I just really thought this might be the one. Well, a one, for a while, for longer than three weeks anyway, for once.

ALAN: Julia went back to applying liberal amounts of old chip fat to her painting.

JEZEBEL: What's wrong with me? Why can't I find that right kind of guy: one who'd actually fancy me.

ROBIN: Julia told her that she just had to work on her self-confidence. She was a total fucking mess.

JEZEBEL: Anyone who says men'll put it any place they can is full of shit. I mean I'm nice, right? I'm friendly, I'm talented, I earn money, I have a nice place- [*Catching herself.*]

Place as in flat, not as in what I just said about where guys'll put it. That's just... average.

ALAN: But Julia wasn't listening. Instead she added a final flick of cigarette ash and revealed her completed portrait of Jezebel. It looked like a wet hamster wearing a handbag.

JEZEBEL: [*Putting a brave face on it.*] Oh. It's great. It'll go well with the soggy tennis ball and mashed potato ones. I'm really looking forward to the exhibition now. It won't be in the least bit embarrassing.

JEZEBEL: Alan and Robin were on the bus.

ALAN and ROBIN are sitting together on a crowded bus. They both look tired and are staring off into the distance not talking.

ALAN has a thought. He's about to share it with ROBIN but then thinks again and dismisses it.

Another thought slowly occurs to him but again he dismisses it.

After a pause he has a third thought. He tries to do some calculations on his hands then takes out his phone, types something and waits. He's disappointed with whatever the results are.

ROBIN: Listen...

ALAN looks over at ROBIN but she can't meet his eye.

ROBIN: [*Finding it difficult to say.*] I think maybe we're out of ideas. We've been working on this for a while now and we've come up with nothing. I know everything else is great but maybe that's just not enough. I know it's just a small thing but it's an important thing. If it's just not going to work in the bedroom then what are we left with? Housemates. You know I'm not someone who gives up easily once I'm committed to something but sometimes a scoreless draw is all you can come away with. So maybe we should just-

ALAN: [*Excited.*] Of course!

ROBIN: What?

ALAN: Tit for tat!

ALAN notices people are looking at him and is embarrassed.

ROBIN: What?

ALAN: [*Excited, whispering.*] A scoreless draw. Tit-for-tat. From Game Theory, the tit-for-tat strategy.

ROBIN looks at him blankly.

ALAN: Maths.

ROBIN: Oh.

ALAN: Both of us are giving people. We're concentrating so hard on pleasing each other that we're forgetting to enjoy ourselves. We'll take it in turns. We'll focus on just one of us at a time, that person gets to request anything they want and we make sure that they fully enjoy themselves without worrying about pleasing the other one.

ROBIN thinks about this and comes to a decision.

ROBIN: Yes. Okay. When do we start?

ALAN: [*Looks at his watch.*] When we get home I guess.

ROBIN: Okay.

ALAN: Who goes first?

ROBIN: Alphabetical order. What do you want? It can be anything.

ALAN: [*Thinks.*] Uhh.

ROBIN: As long as it doesn't involve cruelty to animals. Or non-Fairtrade products.

ALAN comes to a decision.

ALAN: Right. Okay. What about-

ALAN stops, looks around self-consciously at the people on the bus then whispers something in ROBIN's ear.

ROBIN thinks about it.

ROBIN: Sure.

ALAN: [*Pleased, relieved.*] Okay, great.

ROBIN: The table cloth is machine washable anyway so it should be fine.

ALAN glances at the other passengers nervously.

JEZEBEL: And it worked. Doing the alternating thing. They really enjoyed themselves. The next night it was Robin's turn and even though at first Alan was unsure he could pull it off when he heard her request, actually after a few minutes he barely needed the second foot on the ground. And from there they were flying. Well, not literally, I don't think. Although they did pretty much everything else. It started out relatively small and gradually got bigger and bigger: Massages, strawberries and chocolate, the end of the bed, tied to the bed, under the bed, wearing some of his clothes, wearing all of his clothes, on a rocking horse, in the wardrobe, sugar nipples, some kind of system of counter weights, a thing called the captain and the maitre d'. [*Shakes her head in wonderment.*] But then one night while Alan was massaging some life back into his cheeks Robin snuck out into the hall to make a phone call.

ROBIN is talking quietly on her phone.

ROBIN: ...And it's been going great. He's more relaxed and we're really enjoying it. It's really made a world of difference for us as a couple. The only problem is I'm kind of running out of ideas. I've been searching everywhere for inspiration: reading the Kama Sutra, looking for stuff on the internet, going to all the sex shops in town. But to be honest their ideas are all pretty derivative at this stage. I've got to think of something different. I don't want to be the one who lets this fall apart. I don't want to let him down. So that's why I called you. Being a sex line operator you must've heard all kinds of things, right? ...Oh, okay, brilliant. Thank you.

[ROBIN picks up a pen and listens.]

No, I'm allergic to rubber. Yeah, we're both just far too conciliatory for S&M. ...No, neither of us has an HGV licence. ...Alan really needs to let the skin on his knees heal a bit. ...I've never been very good at table tennis. ...We tried that but then there was a power cut and we were stuck like that for an hour.

[ROBIN puts down the pen, disappointed.] Oh. Oh well. Okay. Thanks anyway Candy.

ROBIN hangs up the phone.

ROBIN: Jezebel and Julia were at the opening of an exhibition. In a sawmill. [*Shrugs as if she just doesn't understand what's going on with these kinds of people.*]

ALAN: Julia wanted to leave. She wasn't impressed with the quality of the artists' work. She reckoned they wouldn't know real art if it came up and spat in their eye like her last performance piece.

ROBIN: When Jezebel spotted Carl.

JEZEBEL: Wait. Who's that? ...That man there. The one with the scraggly beard. And the receding hair. That's dreaded on one side. With the leather shirt. And the tracksuit bottom cut offs. He's perfect.

ALAN: Because the Venn diagram of people willing to go out with someone with all those characteristics must surely be a set of just one.

ROBIN: Jezebel came to a decision-point either something had to change or she was going to be single forever. She needed to operationate-forwards on her action-mandate by her own self-discoverables. i.e. She downed a glass of champagne to steady her nerves and walked over to him.

ALAN: The champagne did give her a little bit more courage but also had the effect that when she turned to him to say something about the sculpture they were looking at, all that came out was a very, very loud hiccup.

JEZEBEL: [*Hiccups.*]

ROBIN: She sounded like a sea lion.

ALAN: Everyone in the gallery turned to look at her so she acted like she didn't know where the sound had come from.

ROBIN: Until she hiccupped again.

JEZEBEL: [*Hiccups.*]

ALAN: And Carl gave a loud snort of laughter spraying the sculpture with champagne.

ROBIN: It's not the most orthodox method but it broke the ice.

ALAN: Not literally. It wasn't an ice sculpture.

JEZEBEL: So, what do you do? Are you an artist or... Oh great. No, librarian is a lovely, normal profession. Libraries are very... normal places. I'd love to hear more about that; the books and stuff. Sometime. If the opportunity arose... [*Plays with her hair.*] Wikipedia. Yes, I've heard of it. Maybe I'll look that up on Saturday night 'cos so far I don't actually have any plans for then. Are you up to anything or...? [*Plays with her necklace.*] *Late night* self defence class! Interesting. I was actually thinking of joining a self defence class. Being single, sometimes it can be intimidating walking home late at night. Unless there's someone there with me... [*Strokes her collar bone.*] A rape alarm, yes, of course. But... ummm... I... wouldn't know which one to go for. Maybe you could advise me? ...Okay great. Tomorrow night? [*Disappointed.*] Oh. Right... [*Interested again.*] Oh, yeah, sure, I was actually thinking of going to that club myself. Tomorrow night. As well. So I guess I'll see you there and we can talk about it then. Great. And you're definitely not a drug dealer... No, just kidding. Hahaha.

JEZEBEL: That same evening in their living room Alan and Robin were tidying up after their latest session.

ALAN is picking up tennis balls while ROBIN peels gaffa tape off the sofa cushions. ALAN stops.

ALAN: That was really, really good.

ROBIN: Great.

Pause.

ALAN: So what's next?

ROBIN: Oh, I think I'm done for the night thanks.

ALAN: No, I was just wondering what you fancied tomorrow in case there's anything I need to pick up from town. I'll be passing by the hardware shop. And the medical supply centre.

ROBIN: [*Panicked.*] No, there's nothing... We won't be needing any equipment.

ALAN: So you have something in mind?

ROBIN: Oh yeah, definitely, definitely. [*Looking around the room for inspiration.*] It's... a... surprise.

ALAN: You look a little nervous about it. [*Worried.*] Don't forget I need to let the skin on my knees heel.

ROBIN: No, no, it's fine. Don't get anxious.

ALAN: And one more strike and we'll be banned from the shopping centre.

ROBIN: Yes, of course. We don't want to risk that... sooooo...

ALAN: I mean, if you want to try some drugs, I guess, we could, just give them a bit of a go, maybe, some of the easier ones.

ROBIN: No. No, no, no. I just... I would like... ummmmm... [*Has an idea. Takes a breath.*]

JEZEBEL: To be honest I have no idea why Robin made the request she did. I don't know if *she* knows. Maybe she'd always been curious. Maybe she was looking for a fresh perspective on the whole thing. Maybe she just happened to glance at the Three's Company boxset she'd gotten for last Christmas. Whatever the reason was, Robin asked for a...

ALAN: [*Swallows nervously.*] ...threesome.

JEZEBEL: But that's Robin. She's just a really intuitive person. Very instinctive. When a problem arises she'll always come up with a solution. Guaranteed. Every time. ...They're not necessarily the *right* solution but she'll always come up with one.

ROBIN: [*Rushing to reassure.*] With another woman, of course.

ALAN: [*Still nervous.*] Yeah, okay.

ROBIN: If you want to, we don't have to if you don't want to.

ALAN: Oh, no, no, no. If that's what you want then that's great. Absolutely. Great. Great.

ROBIN: I'm just throwing it out there.

ALAN: [*Trying to "yes and".*] No, you're right. Makes perfect sense when you think about it. It's the next logical step. There's only a certain number of permutations you can achieve before you need a larger sample size to increase the spectrum of possibilities. Is there someone you have in mind? Justine? Or whoever. Carmel, maybe? [*Wincing slightly.*] Sandra.

ROBIN: [*Thinks about it.*] Well, I don't think it should be someone we know because that could get awkward.

ALAN: Yes, right. Online?

ROBIN: I don't think those dating sites really cater for two person profiles.

ALAN: Well, we'll just go to a club and find someone then, right?

ROBIN: Perfect. Simple.

ALAN and ROBIN on either side of the stage pace backwards and forwards.

JEZEBEL: They were both really nervous in work the next day. Robin thought about calling the whole thing off...

ROBIN takes out her phone and is about to hit call but then thinks about it and stops.

JEZEBEL: ...but to hold her nerve Robin kept reminding herself that this was every guy's dream.

ALAN takes out his phone and starts to dial a number but then thinks about it and stops.

JEZEBEL: And to hold his nerve Alan also kept reminding himself that this was every guy's dream.

ALAN and ROBIN meet at the dinner table.

ALAN: No second thoughts then?

ROBIN: No, absolutely not. You?

ALAN: Oh no, don't worry. Let's go for it.

ROBIN: Great. So... let's talk tactics.

ALAN: Oh right, yes, of course, good thinking. Well, it'd be easier to draw, but if you were on top with my leg-

ROBIN: No, I meant... People need to be persuaded to have sex with a couple. They're not like vegetables. What's the best way of... y'know... filling that particular post?

ALAN: Oh. Uhm. Well, to be honest I don't really know. I'm more of the dating kind.

ROBIN: Really?

ALAN: Well, I did manage to take a girl home from a nightclub once but I didn't chat her up so much as I was the only person in the place with a car when a sudden thunderstorm hit.

ROBIN: Right.

ALAN: I mean, I could look at the meteorological report...

ROBIN: No, that's fine. I'm sure we can do this the old fashioned way. We'll just get chatting to people and one thing will lead to another. I'm sure.

ALAN: What should we chat to them about?

ROBIN: Whatever comes up I guess. The economic situation, what book they're reading at the moment, their favourite composer.

ALAN: I'm no expert but I don't think those are the sexiest topics in the world.

ROBIN: True.
Do you have any chat up lines?

ALAN: [*Thinks about it.*] Well, okay, what about... "Hey... How's it going? ...Y'know, with 4 billion adults in the world there's 8×10^{18} different potential couple combinations (an eight with 18 zeros after it) which is a lot to cycle through in order to ensure everyone's maximised their relationship potential so how about we get two of your potential combinations out of the way in one fell swoop?"

ROBIN: Jezebel wasn't having much luck either.

ALAN: She and Julia arrived in the club about 11.

JEZEBEL stands holding a drink occasionally nodding her head to the music.

She spots Carl.

JEZEBEL: There's Carl. [*Tries to wave nonchalantly.*] Hey. [*Turns to Julia beside her, flustered.*] Is he coming over? Just act natural. And don't say anything stupid. Don't tell him about my sweaty scalp. [*Double takes to Carl now beside them.*] Hey, how's it going? You were really cutting up the rug out there... No, not actually. It's just an express... just your dancing. Are those your friends you're dancing with? [*Surprised.*] Oh. Yeah I suppose it *is* more fun to dance with people you don't know and freak them out... Sorry, uh, Julia this is... Carl, isn't it? Carl this is my friend Julia. [*Turns to Julia.*] Oh sure. [*Takes Julia's drink.*] Well, where are you going? ...But we've already got drin- [*Turns to* *back to Carl now holding two drinks.*] She's gone to get... *better* drinks... So… is that a real skull on your neckla- ...Oh yeah, of course. [*With difficulty she takes Carl's drink as well.*] Wow, that's an interesting drink. What is it? Smells kind of like Tia Maria and gravy- ...Yeah, I think the toilets are just down those stairs. [*Indicates with her head.*] Over there.

JEZEBEL is left awkwardly standing by herself trying not to spill the drinks.

ROBIN and ALAN stand by the bar.

ROBIN: Well. Where do we start?

ALAN: Yeah, I don't know.

ROBIN: What kind of women are you into?

ALAN: [*Worried it's a trap.*] What?

ROBIN: Well, you must have some kind of preferences.

ALAN: Uhh, just like you?

ROBIN: Come on, I won't be mad. When you get 2 for the price of 1 in the video shop you don't just rent the same film twice. Large breasts? They're popular.

ALAN: Sure. If you like.

ROBIN: Well, I don't really mind. This is your field of expertise. What's worked well for you in the past?

ALAN: I don't know. I guess I judge them on a case by case basis.

ROBIN: Okay. [*Looks around.*] What about her then?

ALAN: Which, the girl that looks like a wet hamster?

ROBIN: No, behind her, the blonde in the hotpants.

ALAN: Yeah. Definitely- Uh, I mean, sure, if you like. [*Tries to shrug nonchalantly.*]

ROBIN: Okay, great.

Both wait for the other to move.

ALAN: What?

ROBIN: Well, aren't you going to...?

ALAN: Me. Are you crazy? I thought you were going to...

ROBIN: You're the man.

ALAN: Come on, she is *way* out of my league.

ROBIN: Well, I'm in your league. Are you saying she's sexier than me?

ALAN: Not sex*ier*. Just sexy in a different way. I'm just saying that... she looks like she'd be into a particular *kind* of guy. I don't stand a chance.

ROBIN: Well, you definitely don't stand a chance if you don't go over and talk to her.

ALAN: You go over. I thought you were all pro-active-just-ask-them-why-not?

ROBIN: That was with men. Women are more selective. Particularly about gender. If she's out of *your* league what chance do *I* stand? At least you're playing the right game.

ALAN: [*Shrugs.*] Maybe she's gay.

ROBIN: Well if she is someone really needs to let *her* know that. Go on, she won't bite.

ALAN: She might knee in the groin though.

ROBIN spots something.

ROBIN: Tsuh. Now look, some sleezeball has swooped in. Those assholes get all the women.

ALAN: Okay, look, this is a pretty niche market we're aiming for. We need to cover as much ground as we can. Let's just split up.

ROBIN: Okay. Good thinking.

ALAN: Jezebel stood by herself for what seemed like hours but was probably only an hour and 45 minutes.

ROBIN: She finished off her drink and then finished off Julia's drink and then, warily, Carl's.

JEZEBEL: It's a pretty big club, there's several levels and you can easily get lost in there. Robin followed her nose, approaching whichever women she saw fit. While Alan went about it in a systematic approach – starting on the top level with the top woman. They didn't fare well.

ROBIN: This is harder than it looks.

ALAN: Well, now you know.

ROBIN: How are you supposed to segue into asking if a girl wants to go home and have sex with you and your partner after spending ten minutes talking about her handbag?

ALAN: [*Been there, done that.*] You tell me. Look, maybe we should just quit. We can head home and give you some kind of greatest hits package or something.

ROBIN: I was doing so well with that one lesbian lady but she just wasn't budging on the

	whole her – not – being – attracted – to – men thing. I mean, I was willing to meet her halfway here but she was being a real dog in the manger.
ALAN:	I told you we should have gone for that one I found. She was up for it. With both of us.
ROBIN:	I know but… she just wasn't my type.
ALAN:	You're not actually gay remember.
ROBIN:	Yeah, but I've still got standards. I mean she didn't even know why it was called a Qwerty keyboard. Come on. We can do better than that.
ALAN:	It doesn't look like it.
JEZEBEL:	Alan was defeated. It felt like a wild goose chase. Particularly with that one tall girl.
ROBIN:	There must still be some good ones round here somewhere.
JEZEBEL:	Robin however wasn't going to give up so easily. She'd never wanted to have sex with another woman until she was told she couldn't.

ALAN and ROBIN survey the scene.

ALAN: [*Weary.*] We've tried every girl in the place. And some that were just passing by the front door.

ROBIN: What about her?

ALAN: She wasn't up for a third party.

ROBIN: [*Points out another woman.*] Her?

ALAN: She wanted to introduce a fourth.

ROBIN: [*Points out another woman.*] What about that one?

ROBIN points at JEZEBEL.

ALAN: Uh. Actually, you know, I don't think I noticed her before.

ROBIN: Okay. One last try. Let's just come straight out with it. No more beating about the bush.

Pumping, loud dance music plays. JEZEBEL is sitting on a stool by herself pretending to text someone. ALAN and ROBIN approach her.

ALAN pulls the stool beside JEZEBEL out of the way slightly and ROBIN shouts something to her that we can't hear above the music.

JEZEBEL smiles, nods and says something that we don't hear.

ROBIN and ALAN turn to each other surprised and pleased. As they do JEZEBEL pushes the stool towards them but they don't notice.

ROBIN and ALAN start to walk away but stop and turn back when they see JEZEBEL isn't following them.

ALAN gives an "are you coming" signal to JEZEBEL.

JEZEBEL looks confused but gets up and follows them.

ALAN and ROBIN walk off with a bewildered JEZEBEL following them.

ALAN and ROBIN get into a taxi. They hold the door open for JEZEBEL.

JEZEBEL: Oh. No, it's okay. I can get the bus.

ROBIN: Why would you want to get the...?

ALAN: No, it's fine. We'll pay for the taxi. [*To ROBIN.*] Right?

ROBIN: Oh, yes, of course. Don't be silly. It's on us. Jump in.

JEZEBEL: Oh. That's... very generous.

ALAN: No, not at all, it's the least we can do.

JEZEBEL: Okay. Thanks.

JEZEBEL climbs into the taxi beside ROBIN.

They drive off.

ALAN: [*To the driver.*] 37 Highbridge Road please.

JEZEBEL: Oh, that's... not actually... I don't really live very near there.

ROBIN: R-ight.

JEZEBEL: Kind of in the other direction actually.

ROBIN: Alright. Well. We'll pay for a taxi back then. [*Looks at JEZEBEL to see if that satisfies her.*]

JEZEBEL: Oh. Right. Thanks. That's very nice of you.

Both JEZEBEL and ROBIN look away like they think the other one is crazy.

Unsure where to look JEZEBEL turns her gaze out the window of the taxi, but still wary of ROBIN and ALAN.

ROBIN makes signals at ALAN to ask if he thinks JEZEBEL is a bit crazy.

ALAN shakes his head.

Then looks more closely at JEZEBEL.

Then shakes his head again.

ALAN: So, what do you do?

JEZEBEL: I'm an artist.

ALAN: Oh, very good. What kind?

JEZEBEL: Fine art. Some sculpture but it can be hard to get good quality materials.

ALAN: Oh yes, I expect so.

They fall silent for a while.

ALAN tries to think of something else to say.

ALAN: I was reading the other day that we actually drive on the left hand side of the road because when people were on horseback that would mean that everyone passed each other on the side of our sword arm – because most people are right handed of course. But in Europe they drive on the other side because Napoleon was left handed and when he took over he-

ROBIN: Well. Here we are.

ALAN: Oh.

ALAN pays the taxi driver and he and ROBIN get out of the car.

They wait for JEZEBEL.

JEZEBEL, still lost as to what's going on, slowly follows them.

They walk into the house in silence. JEZEBEL stands there awkwardly.

JEZEBEL: Very nice place you have here. I like what you've done with the lampshades there.

ALAN: Oh thanks, yeah.

JEZEBEL: Well... anyway... I should be...

ROBIN: The bedroom's this way.

JEZEBEL: I... sorry?

ROBIN: Up here.

ROBIN walks towards it. ALAN waits for JEZEBEL.

JEZEBEL: The bedroo...?

Realisation slowly dawns on JEZEBEL. She looks backwards and forwards between ROBIN and ALAN. Her mouth drops open in disbelief.

ALAN: Is there a problem?

JEZEBEL looks from ALAN to ROBIN again, weighing everything up.

JEZEBEL: [*Shrugs.*] Well, I guess it'll double my grand total.

JEZEBEL walks into the bedroom. ALAN and ROBIN look at each other, shrug and follow her in.

ROBIN closes the door. They stand in a triangle looking at each other uncertainly like The Good, The Bad and The Ugly. They inhale as if about to speak to each other but instead JEZEBEL turns to the audience.

JEZEBEL: Well, there was no point in Robin and Alan kissing. That wouldn't have been very hospitable.

ALAN: It'd probably be best not to throw this lady straight into the whole girl on girl thing.

ROBIN: The responsibility kind of fell on Alan to step up and be the "event-maker" of the situation.

JEZEBEL: [*Picturing it vividly.*] Alan... slowly... reached up... and pulled the cord that closed the curtains. It wasn't the sexiest thing ever but it was a definite statement of intent.

ROBIN: Then he calmly leaned in and kissed Jezebel. Yes, it's unusual to watch your boyfriend kissing someone else. But an interesting opportunity; to see it in the third person.

JEZEBEL: Next Alan pulled Robin over and kissed her. Which they really seemed to have down.

ALAN: And then it was just about completing the final permutation. Oh no wait! ...*Combin*ation.

ROBIN: Jezebel was displaying signs of nervousness.

ALAN: Robin turned to her and looked deep into her eyes. She reached out and put her right hand on Jezebel's neck with her thumb softly stroking her ear. Then she brought her nose up to her cheek, stopped for a second, and then gently put her lips to Jezebel's.
...It was pretty cool.

ROBIN: And things progressed from there in the usual manner.

JEZEBEL: Piece by piece clothes were removed. There were so many hands swimming everywhere it was impossible to tell who was removing what.

ALAN: Afterwards Robin had to admit that those things *are* difficult to take off from that angle.

JEZEBEL: Once that was done things moved over to the bed... and...

ALAN: Obviously there's no real need to go into all the details...

ROBIN: ...from over her shoulder with Alan kind of across the bed...

ALAN: ...but I think we can surmise that...

ROBIN: [*Cocky.*] I'm pretty sure Jezebel had a good time.

ALAN comes into the kitchen. ROBIN is sitting with a cup of coffee. ALAN looks around for Jezebel.

ROBIN: She was gone when I woke up.

ALAN: Oh. I was going to make pancakes.

ROBIN: You can still make pancakes.

ALAN: True.

ALAN moves over to the fridge and discovers a post-it.

ALAN: "Hi, thanks so much for a wonderful night. I had a ball. Lots of love, Jezebel (from last night (23rd March)" And then she's written her address and telephone number.

ROBIN: Well, I guess that was a pretty successful threesome then.

ALAN: Yeah. It was a good idea. Well done. [*Pats ROBIN on the back.*]

ROBIN: Thanks. [*Takes a deep breath.*] So, what's next?

ALAN: Oh. Yeah. Ummm, how about... just normal?

ROBIN: [*Smiles.*] That sounds good. [*She takes the post-it and puts it in the kitchen drawer.*] Let's keep this though. Just in case.

ROBIN closes the drawer.

JEZEBEL: And the tit-for-tat scheme was put on hold. I think they didn't feel the pressure to be quite so creative any more. They'd pushed the boat out far enough. Literally on that trip to Leitrim. Then one day, while looking for his car keys, Alan found the post-it.

ALAN is holding his phone and the post-it. He dials the number then debates whether to press the call button.

Eventually he presses it and waits for someone to answer.

JEZEBEL: Was he just curious? Was he looking to cheat? Was he just proving to himself that it had really happened? Or was he trying to arrange an extra special surprise for Robin's birthday? [*Realises the audience may be waiting for an answer.*] I don't know. Hello...? [*Struggling to get her phone out of her bag and apologising to it.*] Sorry, sorry. [*Answers the phone.*] Hello?

ALAN: Hi, Jezebel? It's Alan from the, um... from the... well... from uhhh... we met you in a nightclub last month.

JEZEBEL: [*Emotional.*] Oh thank god you've called.

ALAN: Oh.

JEZEBEL: I didn't know how I was going to build up the nerve to. It's all I've been thinking about. I've been trying to put it off but

	really I knew that I'd have to get in touch sooner or later because it's happening one way or another that's just biology I guess.
ALAN:	[*Lost for words, worried.*] Wow... biology... I don't usually have this effect on... I didn't expect- ...well, I don't know what I expected but...
JEZEBEL:	I know. Believe me I didn't expect it either. Obviously. It was just one night and now it's turned into a whole life changing experience thing. Oh, I'm so glad you've called. I really need to see you.
ALAN:	I... I'm sorry, actually, maybe this wasn't such a good idea... I was just wondering how you were getting on and all. Like a follow up call. So... just checking in. Any news at all?
JEZEBEL:	I'm pregnant.
ALAN:	[*Rushed.*] No, everything's fine here. Well, I must run, I'm just on the way into the cinema to see... uh... Raiders... Wait, what?
JEZEBEL:	I'm pregnant. That's the life changing experience thing.
ALAN:	[*Relieved.*] Oh. Okay. Oh, that's great. Thank god, for a second there I thought you were coming on to- Wait, what?

JEZEBEL: I thought you should know.

ALAN: [*Hopeful.*] Because I like human interest stories?

JEZEBEL: Because you're the father.

ALAN: [*Stunned.*] What? Are you sure?

JEZEBEL: Yes. 'Fraid so. Congratulations. You've won the grand prize.

ALAN: Really? There definitely wasn't *anyone* else who entered the competition.

JEZEBEL: No. Sorry. No one else has entered my competition for years.

ALAN: R-ight.

JEZEBEL: So you'll tell Robin then?

ALAN: [*Further realisation.*] Yes. Of course. I need to tell Robin... that I found out you were pregnant... after ringing you up like this.

JEZEBEL hangs up the phone. She looks up.

JEZEBEL: Sorry to keep you. Where do I sign for this?

ROBIN waits nervously.

JEZEBEL: Robin was shocked when she heard the news. It was a total bolt out of the blue for her. A baby is a life changing event however it comes into the world. And this was definitely no exception. But she decided she'd just have to deal with the situation. Life is unexpected as my grandfather used to say. Which was funny because it was a scheduled train that killed him.

I mean she was happy, don't get me wrong, but also pretty nervous. Who isn't when they hear that type of news?

She kept checking the results again and again because she just couldn't believe it, but there it was, in blue and white: She was pregnant.

ALAN comes in the door looking anguished.

ALAN: Hi.

ROBIN: Hi.

ALAN: Listen. I've got something to tell you and I hope this doesn't sound bad but... I just found out... that... w-

[Takes an apprehensive breath but is interrupted just before he talks.]

ROBIN: Wait. I've got something to tell you.

ALAN: Oh. Right.

ROBIN: Well. So. Apparently... w-

ALAN: Actually, sorry, can I just say this first 'cause I need to get it- ...It's just that... Okay. It turns out that... w-

ROBIN: Sorry, sorry, this is kind of big so maybe if you could just hold that thought for a moment, until after I've told you that... w-

ALAN: Well, what I have to say is pretty big too because-

ROBIN: Well, not as big as this. Believe me.

ALAN: Well, wait till you hear what I've got to tell you before you say that.

ROBIN: No. Please. I really think I should tell you something first... because... w- Actually, no sorry, you tell me.

ALAN: Okay. Right. So... w- No, no, I'm sorry. I'm being rude. You go.

ROBIN: No, we'll need time to talk about what I've got to say so you should go first.

ALAN: Well, that's true for what I've got to say, so maybe you should-

ROBIN: Look just tell me, please.

ALAN: Okay, alright.

ROBIN: No wait...

ALAN: You see...

They both take a deep breath.

BOTH: We're going to have a baby. ...How do you know?

Lights down. Curtain.

Interval.

Lights up.

ALAN: Condoms have a 97% protection rate from pregnancy. The contraceptive pill has a 99% success rate. Multiplying that together there was a 9×10^{-6}% chance of two women getting pregnant from the same night of sex. But... there's also 4 billion adults in the world. An average person has sex 127 times a year. If we took the average sex lifespan to be 50 years that would mean people have sex on average 6,350 times in their life. Depending on the survey roughly 15% of people report to have had a threesome. If that were just one of their 6,350 sexual acts that would mean the probability that a given sex act is a threesome would be 2.36×10^{-5}. There is a reported average of 120 million sexual acts a day in the world. That means that according to our figures 2,834 of these will be threesomes. If all of them were using condoms and the contraceptive pill that would mean that on any given day the chances of one of them resulting in double pregnancy would be 0.026%. Therefore, at a very conservative estimate, every 3,920 days, roughly 10.7 years, a double pregnancy somewhere in the world would be an almost certainty. It was inevitable. When you think about it.

ALAN: [*Confused.*] What?

ROBIN: [*Confused.*] What?

ALAN: [*Confused.*] Wait... What? Did she ring you?

ROBIN: No, I went in to see her. The doctor?

ALAN: The doctor? How could you see the doctor?

ROBIN: I made an appointment.

ALAN: Wait. *How* do you know?

ROBIN: How do *I* know? You may be pretty smart Alan, but I think I should know before you do that I'm pregnant.

ALAN: Well, I don't think that... [*Realisation dawns.*] You're pregnant?

ROBIN: Yes! I thought that's what you were just saying.

ALAN: [*Shell shocked.*] What? No, of course, yes, that's what I meant. What good reason would I have for talking to someone else in such a way that I'd find out that *they* were pregnant? That wouldn't make any sense.

ROBIN: It doesn't make any sense that you knew that *I* was pregnant.

ALAN: Well... I... I... uh... I just knew. I had a feeling. I went to see a psychic.

ROBIN: [*Disbelieving.*] A psychic? Really?

ALAN: [*As if it physically hurts him to say.*] Oh yeah. They can be very accurate. Some of them. Sometimes. I mean, when you think about it, even if they are just cold reading that may be revealing things that... you subconsciously... already knew. But didn't know that you knew.

ROBIN: Like that I'm pregnant?

ALAN: Yeah. Well, anyway, I'd better go put the dinner on. But well done on the whole... everything. That's fantastic, absolutely fantastic, absolutely. Fantastic.

ALAN exits. ROBIN is left wondering what happened.

JEZEBEL: Yes, Alan had panicked. But really I think he was thinking of Robin. He didn't want to drop this bomb on her just after she'd found out she was pregnant. He didn't lie, right? He just... paused telling the truth. The problem was the longer he left it on pause the harder it became to unpause.

ROBIN: Alan's the type of person who hates being unfair. He feels guilty choosing between check outs in the supermarket.

ALAN: Hi.

JEZEBEL: Hi. Where's Robin?

ALAN: She couldn't make it. She's feeling a little strange at the moment.

JEZEBEL: Oh no. Well, maybe I should give her a call.

ALAN: No, no, her voice is completely gone. She needs to rest it. She'll give you a ring when she's better. So how are you?

JEZEBEL: Oh, I don't even know. I can't believe this. I haven't managed to tell anyone else yet. Thanks for coming. Sorry, this may sound stupid but I just feel like everything'll just be simpler now that you're here.

ALAN: Sure. Probably.

JEZEBEL: No really, I appreciate it. Some people would have run a mile.

ALAN: Of course not. We'll do everything we can. You'll let us pay the medical bills.

JEZEBEL: Oh no, it's fine.

ALAN: Please, I insist.

JEZEBEL: Well, half then.

ALAN: Two thirds.

JEZEBEL: [*Smiles.*] Okay. Are you sure?

ALAN: Yeah. We can afford two thirds of a baby.

JEZEBEL: Thank you. And thank Robin. Well, I'll thank her when I see her.

ALAN: Yeah, absolutely. No problem. Fantastic.

JEZEBEL: Where's Robin?

ALAN: She's off on business.

JEZEBEL: [*Disappointed.*] Robin couldn't make it?

ALAN: She had to... go talk to her mother... about... hair.

JEZEBEL: Still no Robin?

ALAN: She's very sorry. She really had to go to the zoo.

JEZEBEL: Alan please. I think I know what's going on here.

ALAN: [*Defeated, guilty.*] Oh. Listen, I just paused telling-

JEZEBEL: You're covering up the fact that Robin's angry with me, isn't she?

ALAN: No, not at all. Really she's not.

JEZEBEL: Then why won't she talk to me?

ALAN: She will, she will. Soon.

JEZEBEL: She's angry with me. Is she angry with me? Why's she angry with me?

ALAN: Robin wasn't angry with her.

JEZEBEL: Robin was confused and anxious. She was having a baby, which is really big, and - in the weeks since she'd told him - the person she was supposed to be sharing this experience with was acting all weird and distant. She tried talking to other people...

ROBIN: No, it's going great Carmel. It's just that, I suppose, Alan's kind of been a little distracted lately. A little distant. ...No, no-no, no, he hasn't fled Mum. Not literally distant. I'm just saying, metaphorically, he's not... fully there. Any idea why he'd want to keep me at arm's length? ...No, not because he's showing off his nice arms, Sandra. I don't mean physically. Alan's just been a little preoccupied since I told him. His mind's somewhere else. ...No, not during sex Dad. He's *not* gay. He just wore those shoes once – it was a misunderstanding with the shop assistant.

ROBIN hangs up the phone.

ALAN: ...but everyone seemed to have their own preconceptions about what was going on in her abdomen. Therefore she was looking for someone neutral. Someone who didn't already have a vested interest in the situation. Someone who would just let her and her baby be. And that's when she found the post-it.

JEZEBEL: Hello?

ROBIN: Hi, um, Jezebel?

JEZEBEL: Yes? Robin?

ROBIN: Uh, yes.

JEZEBEL: Oh, thank god you've called.

ROBIN: [*Surprised.*] Oh. Yeah.

JEZEBEL: Really, I'm so pleased to be talking to you.

ROBIN: It's great to be talking to you. You're probably wondering why I'm ringing you...

JEZEBEL: Not really.

ROBIN: Well, it's because, um, it's almost hard to say now, but, well, we're... we're having a baby and-

JEZEBEL: Yes, yes! Oh, I'm delighted you're ringing me.

ROBIN: Oh good. Wow.

JEZEBEL: So you're not angry with me?

ROBIN: Why would I be angry with you?

JEZEBEL: Exactly! That's what I was thinking. Why would you be angry with me? It's not like I meant this to happen.

ROBIN: [*Bewildered.*] No... of course not. How could you...?

JEZEBEL: Right! Oh, I'm so pleased.

ROBIN: Good. Okay. Great.

JEZEBEL: Listen, you may have noticed that I can be a bit ditsy but I am going to really get my shit together. I am going to love this baby and give it everything I can.

ROBIN: [*Trying to stay neutral.*] Oh. O-kay.

JEZEBEL: You know it took a while for it to really sink in...

ROBIN: *It did?*

JEZEBEL: ...but it's happening one way or another.

ROBIN: [*Trying to get back in control.*] Yes, uh...yes, that's what I was thinking. I've been pretty confused about this to be honest.

JEZEBEL: Oh sure, of course it'd be confusing for you too.

ROBIN: R-ight. And... uh... that's why I decided to ring you. I mean, obviously I'm pleased, really happy. This just isn't quite the circumstances that we might have envisioned.

JEZEBEL: Completely.

ROBIN: But we're going to love this baby however it comes into the world.

JEZEBEL: Great.

ROBIN: And I believe, I hope, that maybe Alan and I aren't the worst people in the world to raise a child.

JEZEBEL: Of cour-... wait, what?

ROBIN: Well, I mean, we don't really know what we're doing but does anybody know what they're doing with their first kid? I guess we've just got to child proof the house and take the rest as it comes.

JEZEBEL: [*Taken aback.*] *Your* house?

ROBIN: Yeah, well, it's Alan's house really but...

JEZEBEL: No, I mean-... obviously you're part of this too, in a way...

ROBIN: *"in a way"*?

JEZEBEL: ...but I was kind of thinking the baby would live with me.

ROBIN: [*Perplexed.*] With... *you*? Why would the...

JEZEBEL: Obviously you guys could have it every other weekend or something.

ROBIN: What?! Are you *insane*?

JEZEBEL: Well, let's not fight about this, obviously we just haven't really taken each other's feelings into account here.

ROBIN: [*Sarcastic.*] Yeah, I suppose I haven't taken your feelings into account.

JEZEBEL: [*Not hearing her.*] I guess I *am* being a bit self centred. What kind of arrangements were you thinking?

ROBIN: [*Aghast.*] How about *our* child just...lives with us!

JEZEBEL: What? All four of us?

ROBIN: No, not all four of-... Why the hell would you think you have anything to do with this baby?

JEZEBEL: Well, I have more to do with it than *you* do!

ROBIN: Are you absolutely mental?!

JEZEBEL: No, you're the one that's mental!

ROBIN: No, *you're* the one who's mental!

JEZEBEL: No, *you* are the one that's mental!

ROBIN: No, *you* are the one who is mental!

JEZEBEL: There's no way you're taking this baby away from me you mental bitch!

ROBIN: Away from you?! They don't let you keep babies in the mental home you fucking mentalist!

JEZEBEL: Well, you should know what the rules of a mental home are, you complete fucking mental-

ALAN: And it continued like that for about five minutes until one of them slammed down the phone.

ALAN walks into the flat carrying a cot looking pleased with himself.

ALAN: Hey, I just got a great deal on cots. Cot. One cot.

ROBIN: [*Still angry.*] Guess who I've just been talking to.

JEZEBEL: Alan's heart went into his mouth.

ROBIN: Jezebel.

JEZEBEL: Alan's lunch went into his shoes.

ROBIN: Do you have any idea what she just said to me?

ALAN: [*Ashamed.*] Right. Mmm. Was it about... the baby?

ROBIN: [*Outraged.*] Yes!

ALAN: [*Takes a deep breath.*] Listen, I just paused-

ROBIN: That mad bitch seems to think that she has some kind of claim to this child. Can you believe that? What is going on in her head?

ALAN: What?

ROBIN: Exactly. She thinks for some unfathomable reason that when the baby is born *she's* going to be the one raising it.

ALAN: [*Testing the water.*] *The* baby?

ROBIN: Yes, the baby. You remember the baby we're having?

ALAN: Uh... yeah... that is a bit crazy.

ROBIN: We've got to call the police or something.

ALAN: No. No, no, no. They'd just start asking questions and pointing things out.

ROBIN: So?

ALAN: We don't need that. It'll be fine. It is fine.

ROBIN: It's fine?! Have you lost your marbles too? She's dangerous. We need to get her committed.

ALAN: Let's not do anything rash. She's just a bit confused.

JEZEBEL: [*To ALAN.*] I was totally confused. She wasn't making any sense. At first she was really nice and then she went crazy.

ALAN: Yeah... Apparently there's been a bit of a mix up. I think what Robin meant to say was that... she wants us just to be there for you and as involved as we possibly can.

JEZEBEL: That's really not what it sounded like.

ROBIN: She told me she'd punch me in the neck.

ALAN: I'm sure that's just hot air. And I doubt she's very strong.

JEZEBEL: She demanded she raise the baby herself.

ALAN: Yeah, well, Robin *is* very pro-active.

ROBIN: Apparently she knows a private detective.

ALAN: We've got nothing to hide. What could they find out?

JEZEBEL: She told me she'd set the dog on me.

ALAN: It's a very old dog. You'd easily get away from it.

ROBIN: She said she'd go to the newspapers and accuse us of drugging her to get her to sleep with us.

ALAN: That's... barely a crime these days.

JEZEBEL: She told me she was going to get a restraining order.

ALAN: I... doubt it'd be a very big one.

ROBIN: She said her uncle was a gangster.

JEZEBEL: She said her uncle was a tax inspector.

ALAN: [*To ROBIN.*] It's fine. I promise you if we just leave her alone and don't call her we'll never hear from her again because... [*To JEZEBEL.*] ...it's all just a big shock for her. She needs time to get used to it. Just leave her be for a while and she'll calm down. Okay?

ROBIN: Fine.

JEZEBEL: Fine.

ALAN: But it wasn't fine.

JEZEBEL: What do you mean it's not fine?

ALAN: Jezebel consulted Julia.

JEZEBEL: Take away my- They can't take away my baby. It's *my* baby. It's inside me.

ROBIN: Julia is a classic "tear monger". The kind of person who can't calm down until someone else is getting wound up.

JEZEBEL: What do you mean majority share?

ALAN: Julia reckoned that two parents were better than one and that's how the courts would see it. If Jezebel wanted a chance of keeping her baby she'd need to be in a steady relationship with someone with a steady job.

JEZEBEL: So I just need a boyfriend. [*Unconvinced.*] Yeah, no problem.

ALAN: Meanwhile Robin's imagination was running wild.

JEZEBEL: It was something to do with the plot of the film "Play It By Fear" I think. The one where the crazy woman kidnaps that child.

ALAN and ROBIN are walking.

ROBIN: I'm feeling a little off actually. You head to work. I think I'm going to go home and rest.

ALAN: Oh, I'll drop you home.

ROBIN: No, it's fine.

ALAN: Well just go straight home, okay? Nothing's more important than your health and the health of our baby.

ROBIN: Of course.

ROBIN carries the post-it.

ALAN: She decided to do some detective work on Jezebel and prove that she was definitely crazy. She found Jezebel's address on the post-it.

ROBIN looks up to find Jezebel's door. She looks around warily.

ALAN: She wasn't really sure what the next step was but then she spotted Jezebel's bin.

ROBIN roots through Jezebel's bin.

ALAN: In it she found the assembly instructions for a cot.

ROBIN holds the instructions.

ROBIN: How did she even get the same cot as us?

JEZEBEL suddenly exits her house looking through her bag. ROBIN ducks behind the bin.

JEZEBEL begins to walk and ROBIN tries to surreptitiously follow her.

ROBIN: [*Sarcastic.*] Oh yeah, way to walk sane you crazy bitch.

ALAN: Robin followed Jezebel using post boxes, doorways and a very confused dog as cover. Eventually Jezebel arrived at a library. She'd come looking for Carl but as soon as she spotted him walking in her direction she immediately panicked and tried to hide. In the pregnancy section.

JEZEBEL finds herself in a dead end and spins around to find Carl.

JEZEBEL: Oh! Carl! I didn't see you there. Wow. Huh. It's me, Jezebel. From the gallery. And the nightclub. It's weird to run into you here, where you work, because I was just thinking about you and- ...What? [*Looks around her.*] Oh, yes, this is the pregnancy section, yes. ...No, I don't need a book on... I'm not pr-... Or, actually yes I *am* pregnant. But I have other books that-... [*Growing in volume and perplexity.*] I've known about it for a few months now. ...No, I'm not forcing you into anything. Why would *you* have any say in whether I keep it?

ALAN: It took Jezebel a little while but then the penny slowly dropped. Carl thought this baby was his. He'd been so drunk that night he didn't even realise that he hadn't gone home with her.

JEZEBEL: Well. I don't care if you *were* drunk! That's no excuse. You need to face up to your responsibilities.

ALAN: But he was acting like such a dickhead that - even though it wasn't - Jezebel kind of decided to pretend that the baby *was* his just to teach him a lesson.

JEZEBEL: Oh you think I'm entirely delighted with this situation?! Tough luck mister. This baby is happening. And you are going to be part of it's life one way or another!

ROBIN watches, horrified.

ROBIN: [*Under her breath.*] *What?*

JEZEBEL: I don't care if I have to get a court order! When this baby is born you're going to be there. And you're going to like it!

ROBIN: Holy ffffuhhh...

ROBIN looks around for somewhere to flee to.

JEZEBEL: Well, I hope you don't plan on using that tone of voice with our child!

ROBIN starts to fumble with her phone.

JEZEBEL: Oh very nice. It's bit late for that when I'm already pregnant!

ROBIN stops and looks up confused.

JEZEBEL: I am having a baby, is that too difficult to understand?! Here take a look at the scan! See that? That's a human being that's going to come screaming out of my abdomen!

ROBIN: [*Realisation.*] Oooohhhh.

ALAN: Jezebel had skipped breakfast 'cause of morning sickness and all this exertion was making her feel woozy. She was just about ready to faint when Robin swooped in to her rescue. She wasn't even really sure what this guy had done but that didn't stop her because it was really a great work out for some of her pent up hormones.

ROBIN: Yeah, that's right buddy. You think you're so great standing there all male and unpregnantable. Well, let me tell you; larger breasts are great to look at but tender nipples aren't so hot to feel! Have you any idea how miserable it is to trudge around with your legs feeling like lead?! I haven't had anything but dry crackers for breakfast for weeks.

ALAN: Carl couldn't take arguing with two pregnant women so he vaulted the counter and ran out of the library.

JEZEBEL and ROBIN watch him go.

JEZEBEL: What an asshole. I can't believe I ever-... Wait, dry crackers? *You're* having a baby?

ROBIN: [*Beaming.*] Yes.

JEZEBEL: [*Delighted.*] Oh my god! I thought you were crazy.

ROBIN: I thought *you* were crazy.

JEZEBEL: So you're not trying to steal my baby.

ROBIN: Not in the least.

JEZEBEL: Fantastic.

ROBIN: I'm glad we sorted all that out.

JEZEBEL: Absolutely. That is a big relief. No more confusion.

ROBIN: No thank you.

JEZEBEL: Great.

ROBIN: And that guy's the father?

JEZEBEL: God no. No, no, no, don't worry. Alan's the father.

ROBIN: What?

JEZEBEL: Alan's the... father.

ROBIN: Why didn't you tell us?

JEZEBEL: I did...

JEZEBEL sees the look of horror forming on ROBIN's face and tries to change tack.

JEZEBEL: ...n't have your number and I couldn't remember your address. I get confused about these things. I'm sorry. I didn't want to bother you.

ROBIN: Bother us, don't be silly. We should be helping you. We should be paying for two thirds of the medical bills for a start.

JEZEBEL: Oh no, no. That's not necessary.

ROBIN: Please, we can afford two thirds of a baby.

JEZEBEL: One and two thirds.

ALAN: ...plus another two thirds of course from the previous agreement. Which altogether adds up to 2 and 1/3 of a baby. So there was now 1/3 of a fictitious baby.

JEZEBEL: You're sure you have the money?

ROBIN: Oh yeah. In fact Alan's been working loads of overtime on some project at the moment. He's really racking up the hours so there should be a big pay out at the end of that.

JEZEBEL: You'll have a word with Alan about this then?

ROBIN: Oh yeah, definitely. I'm sure he'll be delighted. What man doesn't want to have two babies with two different women?

JEZEBEL: [*Joking.*] Yeah, I guess we'll just have to share him.

ROBIN is caught off guard by this.

ROBIN: [*Worried.*] Oh... yeah.

JEZEBEL: Robin returned home wondering how to break the news to Alan nervous of how it could affect their relationship, I mean this was some pretty bizarre news who knows how he'd react – if he didn't already know it – which he did, but Robin didn't know that, of course, which Alan knew but he didn't know what she *did* know, y'know?

ROBIN walks into their house. She goes into the living room and returns without her bag.

ALAN comes out of the kitchen.

ROBIN: Oh!

ALAN: Oh there you are. Were you in the living room the whole time? I thought I...

ROBIN: What are you doing here?

ALAN: I came home to check on you and couldn't find you.

ROBIN: [*Guiltily.*] Oh, yeah, I was here. Taking care of myself and the baby. And... not doing anything risky.

ALAN: Why are you wearing your coat?

ROBIN: No reason. I'm a little cold.

ALAN: We should take you to the doctor.

ROBIN: I'm fine.

ALAN: Better safe than sorry.

ALAN starts ushering ROBIN towards the door.

ROBIN: I'm fine, I'm fine.

ALAN: Is everything okay?

ROBIN: I'm fine.

ALAN: You're acting strangely.

ROBIN: I just... listen, what would happen if you found out you were having another baby with another woman?

ALAN: [*Guiltily.*] What? Nothing. I wouldn't do anything. No way. Who said that?

ROBIN: No, no one. Who could say anything when I've been here the whole time? I'm just talking theoretically.

ALAN: All I care about is you and our child. I wouldn't be interested. It would mean nothing to me. They could just shove off, no way am I paying for the medical bills, going to the midwife appointments and buying the cots – two for one deal or not.

ROBIN: Really?

ALAN: Absolutely. I promise you.

ROBIN: Right.

ALAN: I wouldn't even want to know.

ROBIN: Okay.

ROBIN walks away not sure whether to be pleased or disappointed.

ROBIN follows JEZEBEL into Jezebel's living room.

JEZEBEL: How'd it go?

ROBIN: Great.

They sit down on the sofa.

JEZEBEL: So where's Alan?

ROBIN: He... can't make it today. He really had to go to the zoo.

JEZEBEL: [*Disappointed.*] Oh. I see.

ROBIN: He's very excited though and looks forward to seeing you again. Now, how are your feet? They can get so sore, right?

ROBIN takes JEZEBEL's feet and starts massaging them.

JEZEBEL is unsure what to do.

JEZEBEL: Robin, Alan knows.

ROBIN looks at JEZEBEL.

ROBIN: Yes, absolutely. I told you.

JEZEBEL: No. Alan *knows*.

ROBIN: Yes, completely, of course he does. I told him. Everything's great. Don't worry about it. Now, let's not talk about him. Just try to relax. Lean back.

JEZEBEL leans back and ALAN starts massaging her shoulders.

ALAN: Jesus, you're tense. Anyone would think there's a human being growing inside you.

JEZEBEL: [*Laughing nervously.*] Yeah.

Pause. Jezebel is unsure what to do.

JEZEBEL: Alan, Robin knows.

ALAN: Yep, absolutely.

JEZEBEL: No, what I mean is... I think you should talk to her about it.

ALAN: I have, I do. Now stop fretting will you. We don't want this baby coming out all stressed.

JEZEBEL gives up and relaxes further into the sofa.

ROBIN: [*On the phone.*] Hey, sorry, I'm going to be home late tonight, work thing. [*To JEZEBEL.*] I got you that balm I was talking about by the way.

JEZEBEL: Oh, that's so nice of you.

ALAN: [*On the phone.*] Sorry, I missed you this morning I had to run to the... uh... gym. [*To JEZEBEL.*] I looked into that bill for you. You were paying way too much.

JEZEBEL: You're a star.

ROBIN: [*On the phone.*] Sorry, no, I won't be around. I know it's the only night you've had free in ages and now I'm busy. [*To JEZEBEL.*] Do you want to watch another episode of Three's Company tonight?

JEZEBEL: Definitely.

ALAN: [*On the phone.*] No, I left you a note on the fridge, I can't. You go ahead without me though. Maybe I'll see it when you're at yoga on Saturday. [*To JEZEBEL.*] Oh your phone rang while you were in the loo. Julia again.

JEZEBEL: I'll call her back next week. Maybe.

ROBIN: [*On the phone.*] I'll be home late. I'll try not to wake you.

ALAN: [*On the phone.*] Okay, no problem. I'll see you soon.

ROBIN: [*On the phone.*] Bye, bubye, bye, bye, bye. [*Hangs up.*] [*To JEZEBEL.*] Hey, I've been meaning to ask you. I know, obviously, you've got a lot on your plate but is there anything going on romantically for you at the moment?

JEZEBEL: Well, I don't know. I guess there's someone.

ALAN: Oh really. Who?

JEZEBEL: I can't really say. It's stupid of me. It's not going to happen.

ROBIN: You never know.

JEZEBEL: No. It'd ruin everything.

ALAN: Don't be silly. Ruin what?

JEZEBEL is almost drifting off to sleep.

JEZEBEL: It's good as it is. I don't want to lose my friend. And I don't want to ruin what they've got.

ROBIN: Oh, one of those. Well, there's plenty of fish in the sea. Maybe I know someone similar.

JEZEBEL: [*Bites her lip nervously.*] Yeah, maybe.

ALAN: What kind of person do you tend to go for?

JEZEBEL: Well, I guess I'm attracted to smart and logical people, but who are thoughtful and attentive as well. With nice arms.

ROBIN: [*Wistfully.*] Mmm. Yeah, that sounds pretty good.

JEZEBEL: Someone bold, enthusiastic and inventive, and caring, and go-getting.

ALAN: [*Wistfully.*] Yeah, I can understand you falling for someone like that alright.

JEZEBEL: With lovely breasts.

ALAN: [*Surprised.*] Oh. Cool.

ROBIN: Jezebel tried to tell herself it was just hormones, that she didn't know what she was feeling, but deep down she knew that she was falling in love.

ALAN: She just didn't know who with.

JEZEBEL: They say you should never let the sun go down on an argument. There should also be something about never letting your baby come out on a whole load of really complicated lies about it's own existence. I mean it wouldn't work for everyone but sometimes it would really be appropriate.

Robin and Alan sit at the dinner table. Both are tired and don't have much to say to each other.

ROBIN: Oh, I got that DVD.

ALAN: The which?

ROBIN: [*Realises her mistake.*] No, sorry, it was... I was saying that to someone else.

ALAN: Right.

Pause.

ALAN: Oh the early education DVD. Oh, no-... Yes? No. Was that you or-... no wait, that was... someone else. At work.

ROBIN: Right.

Pause. They keep eating.

ALAN looks up at ROBIN eating and is about to say something but then stops and goes back to eating.

ROBIN looks up at ALAN eating and is about to say something but then stops and goes back to eating.

BOTH take a breath and then go to speak.

BOTH: Listen-...
What?
Listen...

ROBIN: Not this again. You talk.

ALAN: Okay. Well. Something... a particular person said to me the other day reminded me of something which, to be honest, I'd kind of forgotten and was taking for granted.

ROBIN: Oh, no, I'd forgotten. I've been terrible.

ALAN: No really. It's my fault. Please. It's hard to explain so bear with me. [*Searches for the right words.*] Sometimes... you do something which you think is going to be a once off but then it turns out to be more than that. A lot more. So this is the reason I've been so tired recently, that I haven't been here so much and please when I tell you just try to remember that I never meant to hurt you, I mean, I'm coming clean now, I could probably keep this a secret but you deserve not to be lied to so-

ROBIN: [*Sudden realisation.*] Oh my god. There's someone else.

ALAN: What?

ROBIN: There's someone else. The absences, the excuses, the detachment? Classic signs of an affair.

ALAN: [*Realisation.*] Jesus, of course; there's someone else. Only an idiot wouldn't have spotted it.

ROBIN: Well, there's no need to say it like that.

ALAN: Well, how do you want me to say it? It's true, isn't it?

ROBIN: I guess so. If that's all you have to say on the matter.

ALAN: Well what do you want me to say?!

ROBIN: With all I've been doing; I have been running around, lying, making up night classes and girls' nights, just to keep what we have together going.

ALAN: [*Sarcastic.*] Well, that's just fantastic. Thank you *so* much. You didn't think that just maybe if there's someone else I might not actually want to keep what we have together going?

ROBIN: Well obviously not.

ALAN: Fine.

ROBIN: Makes sense to me.

ALAN: Well, I guess you'd like me to just go then?

ROBIN: Yes. I guess so, if that's what you want.

ALAN: Well it is, if that's what you want!

ROBIN: Then I guess it is isn't it?!

ALAN: Right. Good.

ALAN waits for something else but nothing occurs.

ALAN: I'm glad we sorted that out then. Nice to know this has all been one big lie!

ALAN storms out into the hall.

ALAN: [*Muttering.*] Two faced... lying...

He goes to the front door and opens it to find…

JEZEBEL: Hi.

ALAN: [*Horrified.*] What are you doing here?

JEZEBEL: I just... I had to come see you.

ALAN: But Robin's here.

JEZEBEL: Yes.

ALAN: She'll see you through the window.

ALAN looks towards the dining room door then pulls JEZEBEL inside.

ALAN: [*Urgent whispers.*] Look, now's not a good time. Robin's really not in the mood. You should go out the back way.

JEZEBEL stops and looks at ALAN.

JEZEBEL: Actually, no. It's just you I want to talk to, not Robin, that was stupid. I know now.

ALAN: Sure, sure. Let's meet up tomorrow. Great, great.

JEZEBEL: Wait. I just want to...

ALAN: Absolutely, tomorrow.

JEZEBEL: If I don't say it now then I'm never going to say it.

ALAN: Good, okay, great. Well then maybe whatever it is is just better left unsaid, so let's just...

ALAN starts ushering JEZEBEL towards the back door.

JEZEBEL: I love you.

ALAN is stopped in his tracks. He looks at JEZEBEL.

She kisses him.

ALAN is shell shocked…

…until he hears ROBIN getting up from her seat and coming towards the dining room door. ALAN snaps out of it and shoves JEZEBEL into the cupboard under the stairs.

ALAN: Quick the cupboard under the stairs!

ROBIN emerges from the dining room and ALAN slams the cupboard door on JEZEBEL.

ROBIN: [*Surprised, still hurt.*] Oh. I thought you'd left.

ALAN: I couldn't find the car keys.

ALAN moves past ROBIN into the dining room. ROBIN follows him.

JEZEBEL comes out of the cupboard but is unsure where to go.

ROBIN: Well, they're not in here.

ALAN: They might be.

ROBIN: [*Snapping.*] Why would they be in here? Who would put them in here?

ALAN: I don't know! There's no rhyme or reason to where you put them.

JEZEBEL goes into the back room just as ROBIN and ALAN go back into the hall still bickering.

ROBIN: They're in the back room.

ALAN: Oh, of course! Why didn't I know that. Well, if you know where they are then you could get them for me.

ROBIN: I'm not going to get your keys for-... [*Gives up.*] Okay, fine! If it means you'll leave.

ROBIN goes into the back room and finds JEZEBEL. She quickly closes the door behind herself.

ALAN opens the cupboard and finds no JEZEBEL. He looks around panicked.

ALAN: Where did she...? [*Panicked whispers.*] Jezebel! Jezebel!

ROBIN: What are you doing here?! How did you get in? Alan might see you.

JEZEBEL: Uh-

ROBIN: Not that that's a problem, normally, as I said he knows about everything and is delighted.

JEZEBEL: Right.

ROBIN: But... he's got to head off on a lifeboat mission.

JEZEBEL: No, he doesn't.

ROBIN: What?

JEZEBEL: [*Caught.*] Um, I meant... No, he doesn't?

ROBIN: Look I know we still haven't met up the three of us but now is really, really not the time because...

JEZEBEL: Actually, no. It's just you I want to talk to, not Alan, that was stupid. I know now.

ROBIN: Right, right, okay, good, what is it? But only briefly because he'll wonder where I am. Is it a big thing? Should we schedule a better time? Is it an action-delivery-point or just a downtime-heads-up?

JEZEBEL: I...don't really know. I love you.

ROBIN stops. She looks at JEZEBEL.

JEZEBEL kisses her passionately then lets her go.

ROBIN: [*Trying to remain in control of the situation.*] Okay, great. Let's put that on the talking points list. In the meantime we've really got to get you out of here.

ROBIN opens the door peeps out and sees that ALAN isn't there. She hustles JEZEBEL out into the hall. ALAN approaches from the kitchen and ROBIN shoves JEZEBEL into the cupboard under the stairs.

ALAN: Did you find them?

ROBIN: [*Guiltily.*] Who? What? No. What? Who?

ALAN: The keys.

ROBIN: Oh, no, they're not in there.

ALAN: The living room?

ROBIN: Fine. I'll look in the living room and you look in the dining room! Like you can't leave without your precious car!

ROBIN moves towards the living room.

ALAN: No wait!

ALAN slips passed ROBIN and sneaks a look into the living room blocking ROBIN's view.

ALAN: Yes, okay, fine. You look in the living room.

ROBIN: And you look in the dining room.

ALAN: Okay fine!

ROBIN waits until ALAN has gone into the dining room before she goes into the living room.

ALAN immediately turns around and comes back out. He starts searching for Jezebel again.

ALAN: [*Whispering.*] Jezebel.

JEZEBEL emerges from the cupboard under the stairs looking extremely worried.

JEZEBEL: Alan.

ALAN looks at her mystified as to where she just appeared from.

JEZEBEL: Alan.

ALAN: Yes. Look. You've got to get out of here. You can even go out the front door now.

ALAN moves towards the front door.

JEZEBEL: I can't. I can't go by myself.

ALAN: Yes, I told you. We'll talk about this I promise. Just not right now.

JEZEBEL: No. The baby's coming.

ALAN: Ohhhhhhh balls. Right, don't panic. I'll take you to the hospital. Go out the front door while I find these goddamn car keys.

ALAN goes back into the dining room.

JEZEBEL moves unsteadily towards the front door.

ROBIN emerges from the living room.

ROBIN: [*Panicked.*] Where are you going? Not that way you'll be seen... by... people. Stay in the cupboard. Just for the moment till we get rid of... distractions.

JEZEBEL: No, I can't go in the cupboard.

ROBIN: Well, you fit before.

JEZEBEL: No, the baby's coming.

ROBIN: Ohhhhhhh tits. Okay fine. Just go into the back room and I'll come and get you once the coast is clear.

ROBIN helps JEZEBEL into the back room and closes the door.

ALAN comes out of the dining room and spots ROBIN closing the door. He comes up behind her.

ALAN: [*Whispering.*] What are you doing? Come on, I've got them.

ROBIN turns around. ALAN jumps.

ALAN: Oh!

ROBIN: What, the sight of me terrifies you now does it?

ALAN: No, I just- from behind I thought you were... someone else.

ROBIN: [*With distaste.*] What? [*Sees the keys in his hand.*] So you found the keys?

ALAN is surprised to see them in his hand.

ALAN: Yes. Yes. Hopefully everything is in the car by now so I'll be going.

ROBIN: No! Actually, I need the keys.

ALAN: It's my car.

ROBIN: Yes but I need it. I'm in a rush.

ALAN: Well, where are you going in such a rush?

ROBIN: There's an emergency at work.

ALAN: What? Have people managed to sort out their *own* lives so suddenly you need to take a long hard look at yours?

ROBIN: Brilliant. Just give me the keys will you?

ALAN: No. I can't.

ROBIN: Why not?

ALAN: You're not the only person that has to work.

ROBIN: [*Dead eyed.*] A statistics emergency? Really?

ALAN: Yes.

ROBIN: What?

ALAN: The standard deviations have come loose on Brian's chi squared test.

ROBIN eyes ALAN suspiciously.

ALAN shrugs, daring her to challenge him.

ROBIN: Well... I'm pregnant!

ALAN: They let pregnant people on the bus.

ROBIN: I'm not getting the bus, I'm pregnant with our child, now will you please let me have the keys?

ALAN: Okay, fine, suit yourself. We'll get a tax- ...*I'll* get a taxi.

ALAN hands the keys to ROBIN.

ROBIN: Oh *you're* going to get a taxi but you wanted *me* to get the bus.

ALAN doesn't answer and instead just storms out the front door.

ROBIN goes to open the door to the back room but ALAN immediately comes back in the front door and marches straight into the living room.

ALAN: [*Through gritted teeth.*] Now I don't have my wallet.

ROBIN goes into the back room.

JEZEBEL: I really think we need to go.

ROBIN: Just five more minutes honey.

JEZEBEL: These contractions are really painful.

ROBIN: [*Half threatening.*] They're fine. I'm sure they're fine. There's nothing to them. Just five more minutes sugarplum. Just till the coast is clear.

JEZEBEL: This is really scary Robin.

ROBIN listens intently.

JEZEBEL: I'm sorry, I don't know what I'm doing. I thought I did but I don't. I can't do it. We've got to call it off. I don't know how but we'll think of something. Maybe some kind of time reverser. Is that a thing? Or a teleporter. They could just teleport it out of me. Right? I think I saw that somewhere. Although it might have been in a cartoon.

ROBIN: [*Coldly.*] Shhhhhh. I'm trying to listen.

They stand in silence for a moment.

JEZEBEL looks down.

JEZEBEL: Robin.

ROBIN: Just a second.

JEZEBEL: Robin.

ROBIN: [*Tersely.*] Honestly. One second sweetie.

JEZEBEL: No, really, Robin.

ROBIN: What?! What?! It's just labour. Millions of women have gone through what you're going through now. Stop making a fuss; you're just having a baby.

JEZEBEL: Yes, but so are you. You're waters just broke.

ROBIN looks down.

ROBIN: Ohhhhhhh tiiiiii-

ALAN: [*To audience.*] Okay, obviously since both babies were conceived on the same day then their due dates were also the same. But only 5% of babies are actually born on the day they're due. The bell curve of actual delivery dates has a high standard deviation. The probability that two children who were conceived on the same day would be born on the same day is... well, you'd have to multiply the chances that one baby was born on any particular... given that one went into labour a week premature... the probability of that event multiplied by... Well, whatever, it happened.

ROBIN: [*Feeling a contraction.*] Owww! Jesus. That's really painful.

JEZEBEL: We should really go.

ROBIN: Yes. We should go. I think I heard the front door. He must be clear by now. He must be. I definitely heard the front door.

ROBIN opens the door to the back room and she and JEZEBEL struggle out each supporting the other.

As they move slowly along the hall ALAN comes out of the living room.

Everyone stops in shock.

ALL THREE: I can explain!

None of them hear each other as they each try to explain things to both of the others – each talking almost on top of the others.

ROBIN: No, listen, I-

ALAN: No wait, don't jump to conclusions. This is-

JEZEBEL: I had no idea that... um... you-

ROBIN: I just happened to find this woman in our-

ALAN: Robin, I didn't... Jezebel, I have never... uh-

JEZEBEL: Nobody told me... about... anything.

ALAN: No, it's very simple... uh... Jezebel I have been very busy lately and...

ROBIN: Is this-? ...this is that woman is it? From the...? Oh I see yes.

JEZEBEL: I suffer from strange memory losses which-

ALAN: No, Jezebel, it's okay, Robin needs to know about my... the surprise party I was planning.

ROBIN: God, I thought I recognised her. Great to see you again. Madam.

JEZEBEL: I thought you knew about... did I not mention... oh, that's weird 'cause I could have sworn...

ALAN: Okay, let me start from the start. My father is a very particular man. Now...

JEZEBEL: I wrote you a note- ...an email. Did you not get it no? My computer... [*Shakes her head.*]

ROBIN: How have you been? Any... anything... any news? [*Changing tack, to Alan.*] Okay, right, yes, obviously we know each other but... she made me promise to keep this a secret or she'd kill our dog.

JEZEBEL: I did not!

ROBIN: [*To Jezebel.*] No, you didn't. Of course not. But Alan wanted me to pretend to lie about keeping it a secret that...

ALAN: No, I didn't.

ROBIN: No, you didn't. But-

ALAN: Listen. My father always tells me... he... he made me promise to ensure that our lineage would continue and so although it was an accident that things happened I had to keep my promise to him by... Wait. Who am I talking to here?

ROBIN: Uhm...

JEZEBEL: [*Has a contraction.*] Look, actually, I'm in a lot of pain.

ROBIN: Yes, exactly. Emotional pain, so in respect for Jezebel's privacy-

ALAN: No, physical pain is what she's saying, which meant she had to take a course of drugs which left her in a state of physical exhaustion-

ROBIN: No, what? No, I couldn't put Jezebel through the emotional turmoil of-

ALAN: No. Listen, she could only have one visitor over the course of the treatment and I-

ROBIN: That's not true.

ALAN: How do you know?

ROBIN: How do *you* know?

JEZEBEL: No, I mean, I'm having a baby.

ALAN: Yes, well obviously Jezebel. We know that.

ROBIN: That's like ten steps ago sweetie.

JEZEBEL: No, I'm having a baby. Right now. So if you two can stop thinking about each other for a second *I* need to go to the hospital.

ROBIN: [*Has a contraction.*] Ohhhhh! Fuck that. *I need to go to the hospital.*

ALAN: Right. *I* need to take you two to the hospital and deliver my children.

ALAN takes ROBIN and JEZEBEL in either arm and starts to move them towards the front door.

ALAN: And so we left for the hospital. I drove.

JEZEBEL and ROBIN are in the back of the car soothing each other.

JEZEBEL: It's okay. You're going to be okay.

ROBIN: Are you okay?

JEZEBEL: I'm okay.

ROBIN: Okay.

JEZEBEL: Are you okay?

ROBIN: I'm okay. It's okay. You're going to be okay.

JEZEBEL: Are you okay?

ROBIN: I'm okay.

JEZEBEL: Okay.

JEZEBEL: When we reached the hospital Alan helped us out of the car.

ALAN gets out runs to JEZEBEL's door and opens it.

Then runs around to ROBIN's door and opens it.

He runs back around to JEZEBEL's side to help her as she struggles out.

Then runs back to ROBIN's side and helps her out.

ALAN runs back to JEZEBEL's side and helps her round to ROBIN's side of the car.

ALAN helps ROBIN to a bench where he parks her before returning back to JEZEBEL to help her.

He moves her over to the bench and picks up ROBIN.

ROBIN: ...and in through the front door.

ALAN: The hospital really wasn't equipped for tandem births

ROBIN: This is absolutely ridiculous! I want to see the manager.

JEZEBEL: So we were in different delivery rooms.

ALAN: I had to run from one to the other changing scrubs each time. It was like spinning plates. One would look like it was about to topple and I'd have to race over there only to be needed back at the other plate.

ALAN finishes putting on a set of scrubs as he walks into the delivery room.

ALAN: How you doing? Everything okay?

ROBIN: Yes, fine. Go and see about Jezebel.

ALAN sighs and starts taking off his scrubs as he walks out.

ALAN finishes putting on a set of scrubs as he walks into the delivery room.

ALAN: How you doing? Everything okay?

JEZEBEL: Yes, fine. How's Robin? You should be with her. Go!

ALAN: But I just...

ALAN sighs and starts taking off his scrubs as he walks out.

ALAN finishes putting on a set of scrubs as he walks into the delivery room.

ALAN: How you doing? Everything-

ROBIN: I thought I told you to be with Jezebel!

ALAN: [*Defeated.*] Yeah, I know.

ALAN turns to leave again. He stops and turns back.

ALAN: By the way, I'm sorry.

ROBIN: I know. I'm sorry too.

They kiss.

ROBIN feels a contraction. ALAN holds ROBIN's hand as she breathes heavily.

ALAN runs back and holds JEZEBEL's hand as she breathes heavily.

ALAN runs back just in time to receive ROBIN's baby.

ALAN runs back just in time to receive JEZEBEL's baby.

Exhausted ALAN lets out a whimper and collapses.

JEZEBEL: Robin's baby was delivered first.

ROBIN: Actually the reverse of the original order.

ALAN: Our little girl, there she was. I was lost just looking at her. But no sooner did I have her in my arms than I had to leave again and rush across just in time to see

ROBIN: The sweetest little boy. He's so lovely.

JEZEBEL: We were put in beds side by side on the ward. The other people couldn't figure out what was going on with the three of us. In fact it took *us* a while, but I think we kind of figured it out eventually.

ALAN: Things actually got a little easier after that.

ROBIN: It wasn't all roses.

JEZEBEL: There was the ridiculous incident with the three baby sitters.

ALAN: Or when Julia and Carl got engaged.

ROBIN: Or Jezebel's exhibition at the waterslide park.

JEZEBEL: But Robin and Alan never forgot they loved each other.

ROBIN: And Jezebel finally found love.

ALAN: Because somehow it kind of simplified things adding two other people to the equation.

ROBIN: Jez's son: Alex Graham Murphy.

JEZEBEL: And Robin and Alan's little girl: Jezebel... [*Proudly.*] Jezebel Fidelma Trollope.

Lights down. Curtain.

The End.